Ready for Any

Janet Wells

National Library of Australia Cataloguing-in-Publication entry
Information on cataloguing can be requested from the publisher
Author –Wells, Janet
ISBN 0-646-44405-0 (pbk.)

Publishing Details
Published in Australia – Touch of Silk
PO Box 433, Capel 6271
Western Australia

First published in Australia in 2004
Second Edition published in 2012

Printing for AUSTRALIA
Printed and Bound in China

Printed & Channels in US/UK/Canada
Printed through Lightning Source (USA/UK)
Distributed in
United States
Ingram Book Company; Amazon.com; Baker & Taylor
Canada
Chapters Indigo; Amazon Canada
United Kingdom
Amazon.com; Bertrams; Book Depository Ltd; Gardners; Mallory International

Margaret Coakes as a young woman

With Best Wishes

Janet Wells

ACKNOWLEDGMENTS

This book is born out of the richness of life in the Kimberley outback and the stoicism of those living there before comfort was a priority and communication a necessity. I wish to acknowledge those stalwarts of our past. I particularly wish to thank my mother- in -law for the huge contribution she has made by sharing her thoughts and memories with me, for the loan of her letters, photographs and written information and above all for her enormous patience in waiting to see the end result. I would also like to acknowledge the invaluable assistance of my mother, Meg Wallace (dec.) who helped with the initial editing; my brother, Harold Wallace, for the use of his computer, my nephew Ian Wallace for his I.T. assistance and my sister-in-law, Pat Wallace for the same. For assistance during the latter stages of it's production I wish to acknowledge the contributions made by my friend Maureen Harkness, layout, my daughter Adele Wells proof reading and punctuation, my son George Wells for the cover design and my husband John for his observations and patience. I also thank Ross and Kevin Fraser and their sister Gail for assistance with Chapter Twenty. I thank my sister-in-law June for her comments and help with the title and last, but not least, I thank Caren Watson of Express Print for leading me through the final processes of production so kindly and patiently.

AUTHOR'S NOTE

The writing of this book has spanned more years than its modest size would seem to warrant. I feel some explanation is necessary.

The idea of recording the story of my mother-in-law's life was not mine alone. Several people over the years have approached her with a similar intention, few if any, had ever lived in the Kimberley, a fact perhaps that went in my favour. In trying to do justice to the privilege she granted me I have read, re-read and re-written my words many times.

I first approached the task by recording, on a series of cassette tapes, her life story in her own words. We spent many hours in her small, galvanized iron home in Derby trying to keep her recollections in some semblance of chronological order. It was not easy. She had a multitude of experiences and anecdotes all clamouring to be told and sometimes we lost track of the current theme. The important thing, in my mind, was to get the stories. They could be sorted out later. We persevered.

The next stage was to type the contents of the tapes, word for word, on my newly acquired computer. A contraption I was still learning to use correctly. They were not the ubiquitous household item then that they are today. I was definitely a beginner.

At that time our family left Meda Station which my husband, John, had managed for ten years. Although we enjoyed far greater comfort there than was available in Margaret's day my task of writing was made easier having experienced station life myself, albeit in a different era.

Living in Derby, as we were by then, I was able to retreat to the luxuriously air-conditioned town library where, for many weeks, I worked on the preliminary manuscript. All was progressing well. When inconsistencies or contradictions presented themselves I was able to call into Neville Street where my mother-in-law ironed out any muddles. I was getting on top of the job when other events, family matters and health issues intervened. Margaret's story was put aside. Five years later, whilst visiting my aging parents in England, I again made a concerted effort to make some real headway with the book. My mother, herself a literate woman and daughter of a former editor of 'The Nation' helped enormously to tidy up my work. Each afternoon, during that last summer with her, we would sit outside and go over it word by word. Every morning was spent at my brother's computer typing the corrected passages worked on the previous day. I was sure, when I returned to Australia ten weeks later, I was safely on the 'home run'.

I was wrong. My small silk painting business took flight. Margaret's story lay, not forgotten, but definitely neglected for a further four years. Now, with the help of a good friend, a professional medical typist between jobs, the final alterations and punctuation have been completed. The long awaited story is finally going to press.

I make no excuses for the belated presentation of this book. There have been other accomplishments along the road and few of us have much time on our hands in this crazy age. I do, however, wish to apologize to the families of Margaret's contemporaries who perhaps have not lived long enough to see this day.

For those of us left in a world of mind boggling technology, where communication can be achieved in the blink of an eye and journeys take hours not weeks, I have one further explanation to make.

The era in which Margaret lived was not sedate, but as vivid, progressive and engaging as any in history. Sex, speed, both kinds, and 'blue language' were not 'in the faces' of the population at large. Certainly there were those who could be uncouth, immoral and thoroughly coarse, but Margaret was not one of them. She preferred not to talk of them and she did her best to avoid them. She is a Christian, a lady of dignity, propriety and high moral stature. She possesses a strong character, always doing what she believes to be 'the right thing' and 'common-sense'. Although she has lived her life among people of varied backgrounds and beliefs, it will be no surprise that her story does not refer to events that did not concern her.

She has told it to me as she remembers it.There may be inaccuracies, but these are her recollections. I have merely added some description to the situations spoken of, to better enable the reader to picture the scene. Much of the dialogue is as Margaret recalls it, although I have included some additional dialogue. I did not want to write a dry historical account of events. I have chosen instead to enliven Margaret's story in this way, to make it feel as real as it undoubtedly was.

I hope it will be enjoyed and that my descriptive input and 'artistic license' might be forgiven. Above all I hope that it will impart a lasting impression of a marvellous practical lady the like of whom should never be forgotten.

Margaret Coakes when a trainee nurse.

DEDICATION

◆ ◆ ◆

This book is dedicated to the memory of Margaret's friend and colleague Sister Alice Hall and to the memory of Margaret's late husband William George Wells.

CONTENTS

MAP

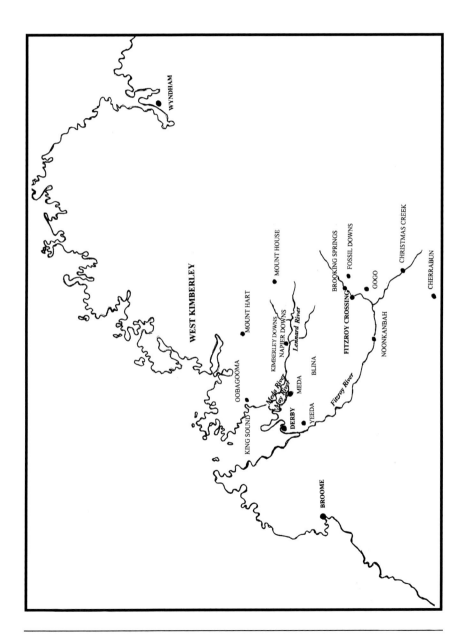

CHAPTER ONE

Flowery Dale

The little girl, Margaret, sat perched on the gatepost her stockinged legs swinging aimlessly. She had been there ever since her mothers' scolding, watching the comings and goings of folk passing along the road. Little more than a bumpy dirt track, destined to become the New England Highway, the thoroughfare ran close by her mother's house and parallel to the railway line.

Margaret liked her eyrie, watching the mighty steam engines rumble by, pulling goods wagons or passenger carriages, sometimes an assortment of each. She liked to dream of the folk she glimpsed within, of the places they had come from and where they might be going. It was one of her favourite pastimes.

Beside the bustle and noise of the railway Margaret liked to see the buggies and sulkies creak and sway along the track. The ladies wearing veils, carrying sun shades on warmer days to protect their delicate skin, and men trotting along on horseback intent on their daily errands. She'd see bullock drays, laden with logs bound for the sawmill lumbering by, the oxen straining against their heavy loads.

Stock were driven to fresh pasture on the far side of the wide rutted track. A small flock of sheep and a couple of milking cows had passed unnoticed by the silent preoccupied child during the course of the afternoon. It was unusual for Margaret to gaze so absent mindedly at the world and not respond to a farmer's cheery greeting. But today her mind was otherwise occupied.

The events of the afternoon and her sore ankle, still painful and feeling increasingly tight inside her laced boot, dominated her thoughts. Not until she had tried to scurry out past the rainwater tank, ducking under the fruit laden fig trees in her bid to escape, had she noticed the injury. The useless umbrellas were still lying in the grass where she had landed. She could not believe how dismally they had failed her in her efforts to fly.

'Why didn't the umbrellas work?' she thought, as she sat, late into the afternoon, oblivious to the passage of time. She had been happy until then, knowing they were kept in the stand in the hall ready for her to use whenever the fancy took her. However after lunch, when Bill had made her so cross, she took the silly notion into her head to try them out. Now look what had happened! Her ankle was sore, her mother was cross, no doubt her father would be told and worst of all she knew there would be no escape. No escape, ever, from this small town, to find a world she so often dreamed of. She had always believed after reading the book, that it would be possible. But the experiment had failed. It had failed so dismally she knew she dare not try it again. She felt wretched with the disappointment.

The sun was dipping slowly toward the Western horizon as Charlie Coakes urged his team forward on his final delivery of the afternoon. This day he was surprised as he approached the neat little house in Malpass Street on the outskirts of town, to see the motionless figure of Margaret, still sitting on the gatepost. Usually as he drew near she would call to him and wave, turning her dark bonneted head to watch him as he approached. A tall, good looking man, dark moustached and well muscled from physical labour, he was a carter, carrying goods from the railway station, making deliveries to local stores, or bringing in the wool clip from nearby sheep properties. He owned four draught horses and a large wagon and many of his tedious journeys were enlivened by the sight of his eldest daughter waving to him as he passed.

Born in Hampshire, England, Rueben Charles Coakes first came to Australia as a sailor on board an escort vessel with the Duke of York, later King George V. He had been impressed with what he saw and upon returning home had persuaded his parents and two of his sisters to join him in making a new life in the young colony. Charlie first found employment in Guyra at the sawmill, where he worked for some time before establishing himself as a carter in the town. He liked living in the high isolated corner of northern New South Wales. It reminded him of his native county, with its moderate climate and undulating green hillsides. Even the wayside flowers, perhaps brought by homesick settlers, resembled those he had known in England. Mullen, marguerite daisies, sorrel and briars, grew in tangled profusion as well as lofty elms, incongruous amongst the stringy bark and snappy gums.

Although he was a newcomer to the district of New England his wife's family was well established in the area. Her relatives, it seemed to Charlie, inhabited every corner of the shire. Jemima was one of fourteen children born to her pioneering parents, ten of whom survived. It was inevitable that descendants of the couple formed a significant proportion of the local population. Charlie sometimes found it daunting to be part of such a large domineering family. For domineering and forthright they certainly were. His wife, admirable in many ways, was no exception.

A strong willed woman, deceptively birdlike and with a dainty fragility more suggestive of French than Irish breeding, Jemima Coakes was the youngest daughter of a large family. She was an accomplished pianist and seamstress.

They had married late, Charlie having spent some years courting the lady he had first seen singing in the church choir. She was a spinster and had dedicated her early life to the care of her elderly mother. She was nearly forty when she finally agreed to become Charlie's bride. Despite her age and late start Jemima soon presented her husband with a family, consisting of two daughters and a son. Margaret was the eldest, single minded and as resilient as her indomitable grandmother, Margaret Starr after whom she was named. She was followed by Vera, or Vee as she was commonly known, and Bill.

Charlie wondered, on this day, why Margaret had not called out to him as he passed and what was preoccupying her active young mind.

The story of Margaret's namesake, Jemima's mother, is one of romance, tragedy and endurance and the legacy of her fortitude and courage is still evident amongst the farming community of northern New South Wales. It began with a covert romance, love-letters left beneath boulders and elicit meetings in County Armagh, Northern Ireland. Margaret Jamieson, the daughter of a whisky distiller and her forbidden swain, Tom Starr, had fallen hopelessly in love.

Tom, a bold young man, decided to journey to far off Australia to see for himself the new colony, said to hold such promise. If he liked what he saw he intended marrying his sweetheart and making a new life, far away from the wrathful Jamieson clan. Tom only sailed as far as Port Said on his first voyage. Having reached North Africa, he felt so fearful his love might not wait for his eventual return, he travelled hastily back to Ireland and married her. As man and wife they then made the six month voyage together.

They first lived in Armidale, where they started their prodigious family. They moved to Guyra in 1878 and settled a small holding called Flowery Dale where they spent the rest of their married lives.

The Starrs built up home, farm and family in their early years, erecting felled timber fences, planting fruit trees, growing potatoes and oats and running a few horses, cattle and poultry. Margaret Starr withstood numerous pregnancies, raising ten healthy children, who in turn assisted with the work. Not always aided in childbirth she, on occasion, barricaded herself into her bedroom for privacy, and got on with the business of birthing alone.

Tragically, her love driven defiance and courage did not reap a just reward. In 1884 her husband, Tom, disappeared while out searching for stray horses. Believing him lost in the bush, long anxious months passed for the young Irish mother and her large brood of children. His decomposed remains were discovered a year later, in a cave, only identifiable by a watch, found lying about his person. The exact circumstances surrounding his death continue to remain a mystery.

Following this tragedy, responsibility for the family and Flowery Dale fell on the shoulders of Jim, the eldest son. Despite the obvious difficulties the family experienced, Tom Starr's widow maintained a commendable standard in the upbringing of her children. Ensuring they attended school regularly, she engaged the services of a music teacher who visited Flowery Dale weekly, to give instruction on the family piano, an activity greatly enjoyed.

Jemima, affectionately known as Mimie within the family, was nine years old at the time of her father's death. A frail child, not yet considered strong enough to make the seven-mile ride to school, she stayed at home helping her mother and older sisters bake bread, make jams and preserve fruit from the orchard. The boys, under Jim's direction, did the heavier work about the farm, whilst the younger children rode daily to school beyond the Mother Of Ducks Lagoon.

During the ensuing years the Starr children grew to adulthood and independence. When Jim Starr, then nearing fifty, finally decided to get married, the event caused a considerable upheaval for the remaining occupants of Flowery Dale.

Jim had become owner of the farm at the time of his father's death. His mother, legally entitled to own stock, was not allowed to be a landowner. Over the years she had become dependant on her son. With a new daughter-in-law shortly to take over the running of the house, the time had come for the widow and her unmarried daughter Jemima to leave.

Jim provided a small house for them to live in, on Malpass Street, in nearby Guyra. It was here that Jemima, determinedly remaining single, nursed her aging parent who died in 1910 following a series of three strokes, aged seventy-three.

Margaret Starr had led a long and arduous life, a world away from her native County Armagh, much of it without the aid or comfort of her beloved husband. Her efforts were not in vain. The legacy of her fortitude and courage is still evident amongst her many descendants, and the strength and resilience of character and Gaelic humour have passed far beyond the cool green hills of New England to the hot dry North of Western Australia.

CHAPTER TWO

'Roslyn', Malpass Street
1923

The chill of evening had crept into the air before the child, Margaret, finally relinquished her vigil on the gatepost. Stretching her limbs she made her way indoors.

" Ah! so there you are at last" called her mother, "Now, sit down and tell me what you were trying to do."

Margaret plonked herself onto a chair near the window.

"I was trying to fly" she stated. Lifting her head defiantly she looked directly, almost challengingly, at her parent.

"Fly!" her mother exclaimed, a small smile escaping her.

"What on earth do you want to fly for? Wherever did you get such an idea?" She asked, fighting to re-gain some semblance of composure.

"I saw it in a book" Margaret answered,

"And I thought if I climbed onto the roof and launched myself off, if I used one umbrella in each hand, I would fly! Fly anywhere I wanted!" Her little face, brightening as she spoke, fell suddenly. Recalling how quickly she had plummeted to the ground, she finished dismally,

"But it didn't work. Not even kind of work!"

"Come now Margie" her mother patted her kindly on the shoulder.

"The Lord doesn't mean us to fly, you know. He's given us arms and legs, not feathers and wings. Where do you want to go anyway? We've got all we want here, haven't we?"

Margaret looked balefully at her mother. How could she say she wanted to see the whole world? Guyra was her mother's world and she had shown no sign of wanting any other, but Guyra was not enough for Margaret. She needed more. To see all the places the train passengers came from, the seaside, the mountains she saw in her illustrated books, the wild animals in Africa and ancient temples in far off lands. Fortunately her mother's question proved rhetorical, for she continued without pause.

"Now we'd better look at that ankle of yours, you silly young imp. Is it very sore?". She unlaced Margaret's boot with some difficulty and eased it off.

Gingerly she felt the injured limb. It was certainly swollen but, she thought, not seriously damaged. She strapped it up with a bandage fetched from the cupboard where her lotions, liniments and small stock of pill bottles were kept.

"No real harm done, I don't think" she told the child,

"Now run along and tidy yourself. We'll have our supper as soon as I've done buttering this bread." Margaret slid off her seat and limped, shamefacedly into the hall.

"Make sure Vera washes her hands too" her mother called after her "Your father isn't in yet, so we'll eat without him" and she turned once more to the task of slicing a crisp loaf ready for their evening meal.

Supper was on the table when Margaret and Vera, hands washed and hair tidy, came tripping back in. Their brother Bill was seated in his usual place next to his mother. The girls hastily took their seats, grace was said and the business of eating began.

The kitchen at 'Roslyn' was a pleasant room, large enough to double as the family dining room, small enough to remain cosy and comfortable. It was Margaret's favourite, the throbbing heart of the house. It had an open fire-place and large wood stove, where iron fountain, pans and kettle hung. It was where all the important activities and trivial events of their daily lives took place, or were discussed.

"You were trying to do what?" asked Vee, continuing the conversation she had started with her sister in the bathroom.

"Fly! but why Margie?" she asked incredulously.

The older girl groaned. How much more of this was she going to have to take, she wondered. She sat in sulky silence.

"Leave it Vee" Jemima urged.

"It's over, and no harm done, other than a few bent umbrella spokes. Let it rest now, that's the girl."

The children, as usual, were sent to bed after having a hearty supper. Margaret's appetite was apparently unaffected by her earlier misadventure. She manoeuvred her sore ankle between the sheets to the foot of her bed and lay watching the last glimmer of daylight fade from her window. Her father had not long returned. She had heard the clip clop of heavy hooves as the horses passed through the gate, the creaking wagon being pulled behind. She lay on her back awake, staring at the wooden ceiling, imagining her fathers' movements as he went about his nightly chores.

It was often late in the evening before Charlie Coakes' working day ended, his wife and family frequently eating without him. On such occasions he would unharness the horses by lantern light, watering them from the nearby well. Winding the windlass to pour buckets of water into the trough he would leave them to drink. He filled nosebags with chaff, bran and oats, finally running a currie comb over them while they stood contentedly feeding. Not until all their needs were attended to did he head indoors to greet his wife.

She, as usual, had spent a busy day. Monday was washing day and she had risen early to get a good start on the weekly chore. With a young boy of five, constantly covered in grime, two school aged girls and her husband to clothe, Jemima found washing day especially arduous. First she scrubbed the more badly soiled garments on a thick glass wash board, then boiled them up in the copper before hanging them on a long clothes line stretched between two pear trees. Her days, always filled with wifely duties, included tasks such as milking the cow morning and night, setting the creamy liquid in large open dishes for skimming next day and making butter from yesterdays' milking.

It was summer and as the fowls were laying well she was saving eggs to set down in waterglass in old kerosene tins. This measure would stand them in good stead during the moult when eggs were less plentiful. Preserving fruit was also of great importance during the summer months and she had been busily making jams, chutneys, jellies and pickles for several weeks. To set her jellies Jemima put them in an empty fireplace, where the draught from the chimney kept them cool. On the hottest days she saved her butter from melting by letting it down the well in a bucket.

Jemima was an adept housekeeper. Coming from a large family she was fastidious and used to hard work. However, she also brought to 'Roslyn' some of the niceties usually only found in homes of the more well to do. As a girl of fourteen her widowed mother had sent her to live with Susan, an older sister who had recently given birth to twins. Susan had married into a wealthy family, and being at an impressionable age, Jemima was significantly influenced by her more affluent surroundings. During that time she learnt, and adopted, many of the ladylike graces that so enhanced her own more modest home many years later.

Her house 'Roslyn', left to her by her mother, was a comfortable home. Comprising three bedrooms, a kitchen and parlour, the rooms were connected by a short hallway that ran the length of the building.

The bedrooms, each with a fireplace, were equipped with washstand, basin, ewer and chamber pot. On the beds were light feather filled quilts, the warm downy padding saved from Sunday and Christmas poultry roasts. In winter the beds were further warmed by passing a coal filled bedpan between the sheets, or by placing a hot brick, wrapped in flannel under the covers.

The parlour, situated at the front of the house, was an attractive room, furnished with a couch, padded chairs and a table. A chiming clock stood on the mantelpiece and several studio portraits, in ornate wooden frames, hung on the walls. The piano was the focal point of the small sitting room where Jemima spent some of her happiest leisure hours. Margaret loved to hear her mother sing. Her high, lilting voice clearly audible in the bedroom across the passage.

Verandahs, front and back, kept the house cool in summer, sheltered in winter and were adorned with rambling roses and a latticed trellis. Outside there was a privy and rainwater tank. In the backyard grew fruit trees, plum, pear, apple and fig, the garden bright with rose bushes, lilac, hydrangeas and autumn dahlias.

While Charlie sat eating his manly sized meal his wife went quietly down the hallway to check the children. They all slept together in one of the three bedrooms. The Coakes slept in the next door room, keeping the third as a spare for the use of occasional guests.

As Jemima stood against the timber panelled walls of her children's bedroom, watching the sleeping forms of her tired offspring, she let her mind drift back to her childhood. Margaret's escapade of the afternoon, still uppermost in her mind, seemed incomprehensible to her. She, her mother and sisters had always been far too occupied on 'Flowery Dale' to entertain such fanciful thoughts as dreams of flight, far less have the time to try to carry them out.

She fell to wondering whether she and Charlie should consider settling a small holding close to town, in the same way her parents had done. They could run a few cattle, sheep, poultry and perhaps pigs. In the times of uncertainty since the Great War, self-sufficiency obtainable from such a holding seemed most desirable. It would provide her husband with a more rewarding occupation as well as ensuring a worthwhile livelihood for their son Bill, when he reached adulthood. She often thought how much her numerous brothers had benefited from their upbringing on the land.

Seeing Bill's tousled curls against the white linen, hearing the soft snuffling sounds of slumber, she paused a moment longer to contemplate the thought of such a future.

Jemima had heard that a small farm of about twenty acres, situated not far away, was to become available shortly. The homestead was said to be haunted, but she did not believe in such nonsense and the rumour, she pondered, might well serve to bring the property down to a more affordable price.

Resolving to give the matter a lot more serious thought before mentioning the scheme to her husband, she returned to the kitchen to find him relaxed and enjoying his evening pipeful of tobacco.

CHAPTER THREE

The Ghost House
1924 – 1934

Anyone acquainted with Jemima Coakes would find it no surprise that the family's move from 'Roslyn' was entirely her idea. In the main her proposals were carried out. Her desire to move her family from their little town house onto a small farm was no exception.

She cajoled, encouraged and convinced her husband so adeptly that within a year of its conception her farsighted plan reached fruition. They had purchased a twenty-seven acre property, known as 'The Ghost House'

They moved in 1924, when Margaret was nine years old, and far from feeling uprooted from her safe and familiar environment, the child embraced the upheaval with eager enthusiasm. It was cause for unsurpassed excitement, her first step on life's long road of adventure. Not that they were moving far along the road at all, for the property was really only a stone's throw from Guyra. But the fact that 'The Ghost House' was to be their new home was exhilaration enough.

Fame and mystery surrounded the farm, causing it to be well known to all those living in the vicinity. Margaret had heard fantastic stories. How the daughter of a previous owner had died from snakebite, coming back to haunt her bereaved family time and time again. At night an eerie tapping would be heard coming from the deceased girl's room, her ghostly spirit troubled and restless. So persistent were the visitations, the police had eventually been called to keep watch over the house to try to unravel the mystery. The press became interested and articles appeared in the local paper. The property became infamous.

It was something of an anti-climax when a discovery was eventually made. The victim's maliciously mischievous sister was the culprit. Concealing a stout stick beneath her skirts, she had been knocking it against the dead girl's bedroom wall. The notoriety engendered by the deception remained with the house thereafter, it continuing to be known as 'The Ghost House' for many years.

Now it was Margaret's new home and life changed for her and her two siblings. It was a time of discovery. She looked out on different horizons, enjoyed different pursuits, adjusted to a markedly different routine.

Her mother ensured the three children all had daily chores to accomplish, including tasks such as cutting kindling, bringing up milking cows from the paddock and collecting bread, meat and the mail on their way home from school. In the hot summer months, when the rainwater tanks ran dry, the three youngsters yoked a horse to the water cart, attached to a wooden slide and went down to the spring to fill it with water. Laden, they would make a slow journey back up to the farmhouse.

Embarking on missions of this kind, the three became good companions. Vera, who was nearer Margaret's age, had always had a lot in common with her, but for Bill the strengthening friendship with his sisters was something new. Their mother watched the changing relationship of the trio with satisfaction. Seeing now Margaret's affectionate mothering of her young brother it was hard to imagine her displeasure and jealousy when she had first seen him as a baby.

"What do we want him for?" she had asked indignantly.

"Can't we send him back where he came from?"

Infancy behind them, petty jealousies overcome, education was now a large part of their lives. Being a little removed from town the children walked and cycled to school each day. They had one bicycle between them and took it in turns to ride or run alongside. Farm children from further afield rode ponies to school, leaving them to graze in a horse paddock during class-time, whilst others arrived by sulky.

School was an integral part of Margaret's life, where all the young of the district came together. Gathering for drill, they marched into the schoolhouse to chant tables and learn their three 'R's. Out in the playground they danced the maypole, played with marbles, hula-hoops and skipping ropes. At the end of the day the pupils burst forth in youthful exuberance to disperse happily homeward.

At 'The Ghost House' the family, working toward self-sufficiency, grew almost everything they ate. They had a good vegetable garden, orchard and potato patch. They ran a few cattle, including a small herd of milking cows, raised poultry, pigs and trapped rabbits. Rabbits were both plentiful and popular, an affordable meat source as well as generating income from skins that could be sold for two shillings a dozen, stretched and dried. Margaret's mother cooked many meals of rabbit to feed her hungry brood, carefully removing a small section at the base of the spine to dispel any game flavour, producing a result so tasty it was barely discernible from chicken.

For Jemima Coakes life on the farm was a bag of mixed blessings. Whilst delighted with the benefits wrought on her children by their changed existence, the financial strains on her and her husband were having a subtle effect on their relationship. Farming did not prove as profitable as they had anticipated. People everywhere were struggling to make ends meet. The tenants, in Malpass Street, frequently found they were unable to pay the rent due on 'Roslyn', likewise the Coakes' had difficulty making periodic payments on their farm. It was a worrying time for many people.

In addition to her financial anxieties, Margaret's mother worried over her husband's lack of enthusiasm for farming life. Having grown up with a family of brothers, all singularly competent and at one with the land, it never occurred to her that all men might not be the same. But Charlie, she soon realized, did not have his heart in it. He did what was necessary, but showed no particular pleasure in his daily tasks. She wondered how long the situation could last.

Desperately trying to make ends meet, Charlie Coakes began taking any odd jobs that came his way. The children and their mother attended to what chores they could at 'The Ghost House'. In time the casual work he took became more frequent and further afield. Something had to be done.

The deteriorating situation at home, and nationally, finally forced Margaret's parents to reconsider their position. Her mother tried to approach the subject dispassionately. It was difficult. She desperately wanted to hold on to the farm for her son to take over one day.

Her husband was also in a dilemma. He was not used to confronting his able but forthright wife on matters of such importance. She was persuasive, capable and determined. She was highly regarded for her compassion and dedication to Christian duty. She was also the legal owner of 'Roslyn', the house bequeathed to her by her Irish mother. He realised his position was weak. The ultimate decision would inevitably be hers and, in Charlie's view, he had little chance of convincing his wife to leave the farm she so dearly wanted to keep.

For Jemima disappointment was difficult to swallow. A rational decision had to be made, painful though it might be. She knew they must give up 'The Ghost House', but in reluctantly agreeing to move back to town, she pleaded with her husband to maintain payments on the farm, perhaps lease it, but in any case hold on to it for Bill to inherit later. Her pleadings were to no avail. 'The Ghost House' was eventually sold. The Coakes family moved back to their original home on Malpass Street. Jemima's dreams were dashed.

The relationship between Margaret's parents became strained. The couple's aspirations were less than ever in accord. She settled back into her old routine of previous years. Her husband sought work further afield. He stayed away for longer and longer periods, until finally he did not come home at all.

Janet Wells

The Ghost House

Margaret was sixteen, close to young womanhood and back where she had spent her infancy, when her father left the family. The future looked dull and bleak. The world seemed more out of reach than ever.

Her mother, anxious to keep a close eye on her blossoming eldest daughter, at the same time wanting her to be gainfully employed, converted a small shed in the front garden at 'Roslyn' into a shop. Here Margaret spent long tedious hours waiting for customers to whom she might sell lemonade, or her mother's jams preserves and whitewash. But her customers were few and she was inordinately bored. She spent many hours reading novels and dreaming of a world beyond Guyra she hoped one day to discover.

Once again a mother and daughter kept house together on Malpass Street, a situation that continued for a further three years. With her father gone, her aging mother beginning to show the strain of sole parenthood, her siblings still at school, Margaret considered ways to try to change both her and her family's situation. She began to think about a possible career for herself. A career that might ease the financial burden on her mother and allow herself to escape the restrictions that had been placed on her.

CHAPTER FOUR

Nursing Training

1934 - 1939

Sister Alice Hall and Sister Margaret Coakes

The year was 1934. Since the departure of her husband, the difficulties faced by Jemima Coakes had been immense. Times were hard, but with her mother's Irish blood running true through her veins, she overcame each obstacle with exceptional good sense and courage. Despite her problems a song was never far from her lips and snatches of poetry often escaped her as she toiled through her days. She found solace in the musical rhythm of words and the courage and perseverance to go on from her nightly prayers.

To increase their meagre income during the depression years she had let the spare room at 'Roslyn', taking in boarders. Frequently her lodgers, unable to pay for their keep, compensated her by doing manual labour. They would repair fences, erect a fowl run or secure a loose sheet of tin on the roof.

When Bill reached the age of fifteen, his mother set him to work ploughing a seven acre plot in which to put a potato crop. They were hungry times and potatoes a food source much sought after.

Of all the events, the upsets and difficult circumstances confronting Jemima, she found none as challenging as seeing her eldest daughter off on the train bound for Sydney.

Margaret, who had gained a pass in her nursing registration examination, was ready to begin a four year training course at Marrickville District Hospital. It had not been easy for her to secure a position as a trainee nurse, despite passing the required examination. During the years of the Great Depression many young women were seeking places in which to do their nursing training. Only applicants who demonstrated a Christian upbringing and who showed evidence of continuing Faith were accepted into teaching hospitals.

Margaret was almost nineteen years old. Despite leaving her mother, experiencing mixed emotions of sorrow and relief, she was ecstatic at the opportunity, finally, to set forth on her first real adventure. She knew her practical mother, who was now nearing sixty, would come to realize the benefits of her going. The advantages of one less mouth to feed. A regular wage in the family. Even the burden of considering Margaret's future, now miraculously lifted, would be a significant relief. Sentimentality and survival did not go hand in hand, as her mother well knew. Margaret, realising she would be missed, did not think her mother would remain bereft for too long. Jemima would soon shrug off the shadows of doubt that had clouded her brow over the last few days and show the resilience that had stood her in good stead so many times in the past.

With a cumbersome lurch the steam train moved slowly out of the station, amidst the usual noise of departure. Passengers waved, calling their farewells to friends and loved ones, trying to catch one last glimpse of those they were leaving behind. Along the crowded platform, jostling on tiptoe was Vera, who had accompanied her mother to see Margaret off, waving a flimsy handkerchief high above her head as the train passed out of sight.

Heaving a weary sigh, heavy with regret at the inevitable parting, surreptitiously tucking her own damp handkerchief into her coat pocket, Jemima waited for her younger daughter to turn back and join her. The two women linked arms and left the platform to find Bill waiting to escort them home.

Margaret was neatly clad in a dark, tight waisted coat, trim hat and stout lace up shoes. The train, travelling at a sedate pace enabled her easily to distinguish the various familiar landmarks that passed briefly across her line of vision. Like a rapid lantern slide show, the images constantly changed before her eyes. She stood gazing out of the carriage window thinking of the new world she was about to discover.

The journey down to Sydney was long, yet full of interest. Margaret arrived exhausted from excitement and anticipation. As they approached the city she had felt unexpectedly apprehensive. The day had been extraordinarily tiring.

She was met at the station and taken to the nurses' quarters of Marrickville District Hospital where she had been appointed to do her training. Here she was shown a room she was to share with four other student nurses. She unpacked her few belongings, made her introductions to her room mates, and retired, early and thankfully to bed.

Margaret soon learned that tiredness and exhaustion were to become her daily companions. The training was rigorous. The girls worked twelve hour shifts, either from six in the morning to six at night, or split shifts with a three hour break during the afternoon and a later finish in the evening. They were permitted a half hour break for morning tea, in which they returned to quarters to make their beds. One and a half free days a week were allocated to each trainee.

On these days they were obliged to attend lectures. They were paid wages of sixteen shillings and nine-pence a week.

Among Margaret's room mates was an attractive, petite young woman named Alice Hall, with whom she quickly became friends. Alice was also a new recruit. Together, as junior nurses, they were given the most menial tasks. One of the more pleasant duties allotted to them was to collect eggs from the patients each day, write names on them and take them to be cooked for breakfast. The less fortunate patients, who did not have their own eggs, were given a breakfast of bread, butter and porridge

During the day Alice and Margaret were given many mundane and often unpleasant jobs. They were generally weary and foot sore long before they went off duty. In the evenings they sat up late and studied, consulting notes taken during lectures attended on previous days off. They joined the Student Nurses Christian Movement. Attending squashes at North Shore Hospital when off duty, they met other student nurses, enjoyed informal social evenings and listened to talks by visiting speakers. Dr Paul White was a young doctor who gave interesting talks about his experiences in Africa, working amongst lepers. Margaret listened avidly to the articulate young man and her dreams of travel intensified.

With the wages she received, Margaret purchased uniforms and text books. After her initial outlay on these obligatory items, and other necessities for herself, she sent the remaining money home to her mother. There was little to spare during her first few months training, but by the end of her fourth year she was earning the princely sum of thirty-two shillings and sixpence. The contributions she sent back to Guyra were a significant help.

She completed her general training early in 1938, moving to Crown Street Hospital at the beginning of April that year. As storm clouds gathered over Europe, in the build up to the second World War, she commenced a nine month midwifery course. For the privilege of this specialist training Margaret took a drop of more than a pound a week in wages, bringing her income back to ten shillings. She felt less perturbed by this situation after she learned that previous midwifery students had paid the huge sum of fifty pounds to do the same course.

The midwifery students at Crown Street worked only eight hour shifts, from five in the morning until one in the afternoon, or late shift, from one until nine in the evening. There were no days off for the duration of the course, which included some district nursing in the slum regions of Surrey Hills.

Margaret, always used to fastidious cleanliness, found her experiences of District Nursing the most enduring of memories. Called out on a roster system, the nurses wore black hat, coat, shoes and stockings, for all visits. They carried a black bag containing essential equipment for a home delivery and had ten minutes, from the time of their call, to leave the ward, change their uniforms, collect the bag and be out to the waiting taxi.

Arriving at the appointed location, district nurses usually found a small crowd of onlookers eagerly waiting to direct them to the labouring woman's door. Once inside, the inquisitive audience safely shut out, the sisters would assess the patient's condition.

Using a discarded beer bottle, or similar receptacle, they would place a candle in it and test the woman's urine, holding it in a test-tube over the flame.

When the patient's initial observations were done, they ensured the copper was alight, providing them with boiling water for sterilization purposes, and that an adequate newspaper pad had been made for the patient to lie on for the birth. Then they placed their own waterproof sheet on the woman's bed.

During the hours of labour regular phone calls were made to the hospital, to report the patient's progress. The tuppenny calls were made from a nearby phone box, invariably overlooked by interested neighbours. Inquisitive onlookers were often a problem for the sisters who would sometimes place hessian bags over downstairs windows, to keep out prying eyes. Deliveries were frequently made by lantern light, the slum dwellers, often unable to pay their electricity bills.

After delivery, once the patient was settled and not bleeding, the baby was bathed. Case notes were then written in a book provided for the purpose. The placenta, wrapped securely in newspaper, was taken back with them in the taxi for the senior sister at the hospital to check.

It was sometimes necessary for the district nurses to remain all night with a woman in labour. They only transferred patients to hospital if unexpected complications arose. Much support and assistance was provided by the nurses in the poorer quarters of Sydney at such times and Margaret found the experiences satisfying and worthwhile. She was interested to see how others lived and enjoyed a feeling of helping people less fortunate than herself.

While Margaret was doing her training at Crown Street, her friend Alice Hall was doing a similar course at Paddington, but the friendship they had struck up during their four years at Marrickville remained lasting. The evenings spent at North Shore Hospital and the talks on Africa by Dr Paul White were not forgotten.

Margaret's resolve to go to that dark continent and work amongst lepers had not lessened. Now, at the completion of her training, she felt she at last had the necessary credentials to do what she had so long dreamed of. She returned to Guyra, qualified, keen and as full of a need for adventure as ever, to inform her mother of her intentions.

CHAPTER FIVE

The Australian Inland Mission

1939

After the initial delight of Margaret's homecoming her mother's mood suddenly changed. The reaction to her proposal to travel overseas was dramatic and unexpected. She was not at all happy at her daughter's intention to follow her dream of nursing amongst the leper colonies of Africa. When Margaret, trying to soothe her mother's offended emotions, pointed out that such work would help fulfill her need to do her Christian duty, Jemima was no less distressed.

Unlike her own mother who had travelled, newly married, from Ireland to Australia almost seventy years earlier, Margaret's mother had never left the district of New England. With the exception of one brief visit to Sydney during Margaret's early nursing days, a disastrous experience undertaken against her will, Jemima seldom travelled further afield than Armidale, some twenty miles from her home. She was not an adventurous woman.

Unable to conceive an idea more apalling than to lose her cherished eldest daughter to a place of such unknown horror and hardship, Jemima's anguish was intense. Was this the result of a strict Christian upbringing, she wondered, and was it really necessary for Margaret to travel half a world away to satisfy her sense of duty? Jemima had always maintained a strong belief in helping the needy and less fortunate, instilling her ideas on her three children. Was this now to result in the loss of her dependable daughter to Christian service overseas, amongst the world's most impoverished and wretched?

Her mother's despair, so evident to Margaret, gave her pause to reconsider her decision. She tried her best to reassure her, telling her that the risks were minimal, the safeguards real, but to no avail. In the face of such opposition Margaret's enthusiasm began to wane. She found it impossible to maintain her determination and commitment amidst such distress. It soon became apparent that nothing would console her mother other than a promise to remain within Australia.

Disappointed though she was at the thought of relinquishing her chosen course, Margaret reluctantly began considering other options open to her. Options that would still enable her to fulfill her own desires, yet maintain a promise to her distraught parent not to leave the continent.

About this time her long time friend Alice Hall, who had joined the Australian Inland Mission, founded by the Reverend John Flynn, was looking for a colleague to go into the outback to open a new hospital. Alice asked Margaret to accompany her. Margaret readily agreed to this suggestion which seemed to be a good solution to her problems, so she too joined the Australian Inland Mission.

In 1939 Sisters Alice Hall and Margaret Coakes were appointed to open the new hospital being built by the A.I.M. at Fitzroy Crossing, a remote township in the Kimberley region of Western Australia. Margaret's mother could never have dreamed, when extracting that promise to remain in Australia, that fate would nevertheless take her daughter so terrifyingly far afield.

No sooner had the two young women committed themselves to the A.I.M. than the world was plunged into the Second World War. Suffering agonies of indecision, Margaret and Alice endeavoured to decide in which direction their line of duty lay. Should they proceed with the new mission hospital or would their duty be better served by joining the Nurses Corporation? Finally they both decided on the latter.

When they informed the Australian Inland Mission the organization adamantly refused them leave to join the war effort, stating that they had both signed up and were therefore irrevocably committed to the task now allotted to them. Having no choice the two nursing sisters busied themselves with preparations for their forthcoming journey to the far side of the continent.

First they set out to Anthony Hordens Store in Sydney with a requisition for goods to establish the small outpost hospital to which they had been designated. The items procured were packed up and despatched, ahead of the nurses, to Western Australia. Then they attended meetings and introductions to various A.I.M. personnel, its benefactors and other well wishers, all of whom had, it seemed, some snippet of advice to bestow on the two young women recently recruited to their ranks.

Family farewells had followed, with a further set of instructions. This time Margaret's mother, taking her daughter aside, had emphasised the necessity of conducting herself with good sense and decorum, no matter how primitive or remote her surroundings might be. She reminded her to always do her Christian duty, avoid the evils of the world, gambling and the advances of unworthy men, as well as shun all forms of alcohol except for medicinal purposes. She was further instructed to keep in touch with the family and above all to use common sense as her guide in the face of whatever adversity she might ultimately encounter.

At last, in October 1939 she and Alice boarded the steam train at Sydney's Central Station bound for Perth in far off Western Australia.

"If you die over there Marge, we'll bring your body back!" Vera had whispered dramatically just before departure. 'Just as if we were going to the war instead of a wonderful adventure', thought Margaret.

Their journey across the vast continent was broken first with a stopover in Melbourne, where they were met by members of the Australian Inland Mission who dutifully showed them the sights of the city. They were cared for in a similar manner upon their arrival in Adelaide, but the highlight of the train journey for both young women had been their introduction to Daisy Bates whom they had met at Ooldea, a tiny railway siding on the Nullabor Plain.

When their train at last arrived in Perth they were pleased to be met by John Flynn. With the breadth of Australia between them and their loved ones and a sea of strange faces about them his familiar appearance was a welcome sight.

(Margaret's first letter home, written during her journey across Australia in October 1939 in the train 'Spirit of Progress')

Dear Mum & Bill,

Well we left Sydney last night amidst great excitement. About twenty four people saw us off, and others sent their apologies. Intense excitement and we were loaded with beautiful fruit, chocolates, preserved ginger, flowers, dates, cake and books. We had our work cut out saying goodbye to everyone.

Then we settled into the train, the conductor made up our beds and fixed us up in like a little room all to ourselves. I couldn't sleep I was so excited. The bed was comfortable, and rubber mattresses, we had our own wash basin and little cupboards for our clothes.

When we changed at the border of N.S.W. and Victoria into the Spirit of Progress while our luggage was being transferred, we breakfasted on porridge, fish and chips, toast and tea for 2/6. Into the train, Spirit of Progress, a luxurious piece of work travelling between sixty and seventy miles per hour, hence the writing. The country is marvelous green and cattle almost hidden by grass. Lots of sheep and lambs in good condition. A verdant green stretches over the hills.

We are now within two hours of Melbourne. It looks like rain. Fortunately I have my rain coat and umbrella packed in my rig. We have messages to deliver and names to remember all the way. I will have to leave this till tonight after we have met the people of Melbourne- - - - - -

- - - - Arrived safely in Melbourne. We were met by Miss Hartnell, taken to the Hotel Victoria, the largest temperance hotel in Melbourne. After a wash we lunched with Miss Hartnell and Miss Ross. Then had a walk round Melbourne and a look at St. Paul's Church of England, a huge church, well kept. Also saw Scots church. Had afternoon tea with the Melbourne office team, wherein they welcomed us and we had a few speeches. Then we were interviewed by a Melbourne press reporter (woman). So whether we will appear in print I do not know.

Then Mr & Mrs Poole drove us all round Melbourne, over the Yarra River where we saw the various school boys rowing the boats, practising. The streets are wider, the trams quieter, the air quite fresh, lots of parks and gardens. The people (women) do not seem to use as much make up and are quieter types. Each street has a little street of the same name.

We visited the Town Hall and were shown all over the same. Beautiful rooms and upholstery. Had a guide to show us round.

Sat in the Lord Mayor's chair and signed our names in the visitors book. All for nothing. Are now about to retire to bed as Miss Elder is taking us out tomorrow and at night we are having dinner with Mrs Flynn and Miss Strachan. Then we will be on the train, eating and sleeping from 7 p.m. Wednesday evening till Saturday dinner time.

Don't think I mentioned in the rush, the fowl was beautifully tender and we had a lot of meals off it, and the puddings of course were delicious.

We have hot and cold water in our bedroom here. Will leave this open and may add a few words in the morning, if not will just post it.

Love
Margie.

PS We are very matter of fact, in Melbourne, for the first time; meeting strangers, having meals. Staying at one of the best hotels and being interviewed by the press and treating it like a drink of water and hardly noticing it. Send this letter on to Vera. You can exchange letters.

Best Love Margie.

Further extract from letters home

> *We looked up and down the station and saw Reverend Flynn, so we both rushed up and grabbed him. I don't know what he thought.*
>
> *He had Mr Berry and Black with him. We hardly drew breath when a newspaper reporter rushed up to us and wanted our story. However Rev. John told him to come round to the church offices after which he did and we are in the paper this morning.'*

♦ ♦ ♦

In Perth they were taken to lodgings. Friends and members of the Australian Inland Mission took them out daily to lunch at their various homes. They were introduced to Senator Agnes Robeton, Beryl Grant, the Reverend George Tulloch and his daughter Enid Tulloch, and many other West Australians.

Whilst in Perth and before embarking on the next leg of their journey to the far North the two nursing sisters were obliged to attend a 'setting aside' ceremony at St. Andrews Church. Embarassed at the prospect of having to be seated on the dais at the front of the church they conspired to arrive a little behind schedule, in the hope that they might be able to sit elsewhere. Their failure to be punctual, as well as being out of character, did the pair little good. To their further discomfort, they were firmly led to the dais in the face of a full and expectant congregation.

Bestowed with blessings and prayers for their mission, Alice and Margaret were taken to Fremantle to board the Koolama. Neither had sailed before and both girls experienced the misery of seasickness within hours of departure.

They were woken in the early hours of the morning by a sharp knock on their cabin door and were surprised to receive an invitation to drink early morning tea in the captain's cabin. Margaret was dubious about accepting this.

"I think it seems a very shifty sort of thing to do" Margaret grumbled as she hurriedly dressed. Still feeling weak and mildly nauseous Alice retorted sharply

"What, don't you think his intentions are honourable Margaret? Why in all probability he only wants to show us some point of interest we may be passing."

And so it had proved to be.

When they disembarked at Port Hedland almost a week later the heat seemed intense. Dr. Vickers met them and took them to lunch with matron King. Dr. Vickers was in charge of the little hospitals already established in Broome, Derby and Wyndham. Their departure from the hot iron mining town later that afternoon was a welcome relief from the oppressive heat on shore.

Their next port of call was Broome, a tiny town with a few old shops and wonderful clear blue green water, a colour they remembered wistfully as their ship sailed down the King Sound the following day. In Derby Alice and Margaret gathered up their few belongings and left the cabin for the last time. This was their port of disembarkation. The second leg of the journey was almost complete.

Dr. Farragher, an Englishman, Matron Hack and Mr. Ray Russ of Mongers and Co. were on the jetty to meet them. Margaret wondered at Mr. Russ' presence but soon realised he was providing the vehicle that was to convey them all to the hospital where they were to be accommodated. Matron Hack, lending her bed to Alice, slept on the floor. Margaret was given a hospital bed on the verandah. The hospital consisted of a four bed men's ward on a verandah, a single room for maternity cases, a second verandah ward for female patients and the matron's room. Margaret and Alice made the acquaintance of the hospital staff. Apart from Matron Hack they were introduced to Sister Stewart, the orderly Charles GoLightly and the cook, Olive Hansen.

Staying in Derby over the following few days was a mixed experience. Margaret rose early each morning, woken by the hot October sun shining down on her. They were taken out to visit the Leprosarium in the back of an old red truck with a splintery floorboard. Little was then known about leprosy. Margaret wondered about the cleanliness of the conveyance in which they travelled. They drove out across the marsh to the small settlement situated on a pindan point a few miles from the town. There they were greeted by the superintendant Mr Walsh and his wife. After luncheon had been served Alice and Margaret were shown around. The lepers were being cared for by three nuns who were blood sisters. Mother Gertrude, Sister Mathews and Sister Green. Some of the patients were sleeping, others were making bread. To Margaret's surprise a large communal canvas waterbag hung on the verandah. She was most interested in the Leprosarium and the work of the dedicated care givers. She recalled her earlier dreams of working amongst the lepers of Africa.

On their return to Derby the girls were taken to the Native Hospital where Mrs. Ulrich was to give them afternoon tea. This was not a success. Firstly, because they had arrived late, secondly because they would not eat the jam tarts and goats cream she had prepared for them. These tasted strongly of the Leichardt Pines upon which the goats fed. It was a relief for the young visitors to escape to the sanctuary of the hospital.

Their final evening in Derby was spent out on the marsh where Charles GoLightly cooked steak, potatoes and onions, roasted in the ashes of a camp fire. Margaret's sense of decorum was happily in tact on this occasion, for she and Alice were merely bystanders to the romantic attentions he was paying Sister Stewart. Together the enamoured couple stood on a tree stump in the moonlight singing duets, a ridiculous display of frivolity to the mind of the plain thinking young woman from Guyra. The evening under the stars, sitting on the mud flats of Derby amongst the mosquitos and sandflies was not at all to her taste.

They left Derby the following morning by plane. Margaret thinking, just prior to take off, that this was the last they would see of civilization for a long time, suddenly banged urgently on the door of the aircraft. She glanced at their pilot, Jimmy Branch, saying briefly

"I've forgotten something." She banged on the door again and presently it was re-opened.

"Could we have a box of matches please" she asked. Puzzled expressions were exchanged between the bystanders but presently she was handed some matches.

"Thank you. Thank you so much" she beamed, then to Jimmy Branch she nodded,

"Yes, I'm sorry. We're ready to go now." They sped across the dry mudflats behind Mongers Agency and lifted up into the clear October sky. Circling briefly over the town they headed out across the vast emptiness of the outback in the direction of Fitzroy Crossing.

Not having flown before, the sensation of lifting, dipping and occasionally losing her middle were at once exhilarating, yet unnerving for Margaret. Her enjoyment was soon spoilt by the effect on her eardrums, the pain of which was excruciating. She was amazed to find, on landing at Noonkenbah Station, that they had not perforated.

Grace and Bill Henwood, managers of Noonkenbah Sheep Station, served the travellers morning tea. Margaret was intrigued to see ice cubes laid around the butter to save it from melting. There was much to learn about living in this interminable heat, she thought, and would bear the tip in mind.

Refreshed from their brief interval on the ground Jimmy Branch once again guided his small aeroplane into the sky and set his course. Their long journey was almost over. Alice and Margaret looked at one another. There was nothing to be seen from the small windows, only mile upon mile of flat, dry landscape with an occasional small rocky outcrop. Away to one side was a distant range, but nowhere was there any sign of habitation.

Presently they began to descend. A line of taller timber snaked its way across the landscape. A river perhaps, Margaret thought, but there was no glimmer of water. Quite suddenly the ground seemed much closer and in a few short moments the plane touched down on a small airstrip and lumbered to a standstill.

A few dwellings were visible in the distance. The flat ground shimmered and blurred in the heat and two or three men in white shirts, wearing wide brimmed hats, stood looking curiously at the plane as the young women clambered out.

'So this is it!' thought Margaret. 'Fitzroy Crossing, Western Australia, here I am at last'.

One of the men stepped forward to greet the girls.

"Bert Lockhart" he said extending his hand.

"I'm the linesman. I've been sent down to pick you up. The postmaster was meant to, but he's a bit under the weather I'm afraid" he remarked cheerfully.

"The races are on, see" he added, as if in explanation.

They walked towards Mr. Lockhart's car. Margaret felt the eyes of the other onlookers following them as they made their way across the hot ground.

"Who are those people?" she asked, indicating the men clad in silk shirts and big hats.

"Oh, them. Well on the left is Sam Thomas and that's George Wells in the————"

"But what are they here for?" she interrupted him.

"Oh I see, - just to 'ave a look I guess" he laughed.

"There's been a lot of talk 'bout you girls round here, 'specially since they sent your photos over" he explained.

"Not many white women come to these parts, especially not marriageable material. Quite a stir you'll cause I bet."

Margaret cast an outraged look at her companion. Then, with shoulders back and head held high, she walked with supreme dignity to the waiting car without casting another glance behind her.

"Hop in girls" their escort said cheerfully.

"I'll run you to my place. The Mrs. has got lunch all lined up for you. Ted Millard from GoGo, he's the kinda local chairman of the A.I.M., will pick yous up this arvo' and run you out to the station."

"Whatever for?" questioned Margaret suspiciously

"Ah well, the hospital isn't quite finished see" Bert Lockhart told her,

"so Ted's arranged for you to stay out at GoGo till Benn Hargraves completes the building." Then seeing the defiant look on Margaret's face he added quickly

"It's all right girls. Ted is a respectable married man and highly thought of round here."

Before Margaret could reply Alice nudged her sharply, saying to Mr. Lockhart

"Well that is very kind indeed of him. How long is the hospital likely to take do you think?"

"Oh, only a matter of days I believe." he responded

"Well, here we are. Out you hop. I'll just get your bags from the back." and so doing they made their way inside to be greeted by his wife.

Luncheon was a surprisingly elegant affair. Mrs. Lockhart seemed to have dressed smartly for the occasion. She was wearing a more modern frock than either of the girls possessed, and was also adorned with lipstick. Far from wearing dresses to the ground, as Margaret had half expected, the ladies of Fitzroy appeared to be very much in fashion. To Margaret's surprise fresh lettuce was served with the meal. She learnt later that this delicacy had been flown in on the plane with them. She was pleased to find things were not as primitive as she had expected.

After lunch the two girls were driven out to GoGo. Crossing the Fitzroy River it was only a short journey to the cattle station where they were to stay. On their arrival they were shown to their room by Ted Millard who apologized for his wife's absence explaining that she was away in Perth.

They were shown to their room on a covered verandah where Mr Millard suggested they settle in and enjoy a short siesta. It was the usual practice on the station, he told them, to sleep during the hottest part of the afternoon, when work permitted. The remainder of the day was spent acquainting themselves with their surroundings. Ted Millard showed them over the homestead before leaving them to wander freely where they chose. They all met again for the evening meal, which was served quite early, and retired soon afterwards to their beds.

CHAPTER SIX

Fitzroy Crossing

1939

A lice awoke with a start. In the still quietness of the verandah, her friend's muffled shriek had sounded appallingly loud. As she looked across at the low iron framed bed alongside her she could see Margaret sitting bolt upright. Breathing rapidly, she was holding the light cotton sheet close under her chin as she stared searchingly towards the shadowy corners of their makeshift bedroom.

"Whatever is it?" Alice asked, concerned to see the usually composed expression of her staunch companion given way to one of indignation and alarm.

"Oh Alice - sorry! Did I wake you? I didn't know I'd called out." said Margaret.

Quickly regaining her composure she gave a self conscious laugh. Alice thought there was little humour in the sound and asked again what was troubling her friend.

"It was nothing Alice. Don't worry" Margaret told her.

"Just the wind in this canvas curtain. It blew onto me and well - I thought it was - someone." she finished rather lamely.

"Someone?" Questioned Alice.

"Like who?"

" Oh, I don't know" said Margaret shortly.

"I just don't think it's right us being out here at GoGo with Mrs

Millard away. I wouldn't have agreed to come if I'd known we were to be the only women on the station."

"Oh, I see!" said Alice, adding matter of factly

"And where else would we have stayed do you think? Mr Millard seems the perfect gentleman and I'm sure it's most kind of him to put us up until the hospital is finished. It's those young fellows that met the plane in Fitzroy who have unnerved you, I'll bet. Don't be so touchy and go back to sleep. We'll get used to the way things are up here in time. We're both overtired from the journey and we've got to be up for breakfast at 5 o'clock." Alice told her firmly.

Margaret reluctantly conceded that her friend was right. She was overtired and it was so dreadfully hot she found it hard to sleep. She rolled over and closed her eyes firmly, shutting out the pale tropical night and refusing to look at the starry heavens beyond the verandah railing. She was angry with herself that sleep still had not overtaken her. Her distrust of male intentions had twice caused Alice to reproach her since the outset of their mission. She must take a grip on herself and keep her suspicions better concealed in future she concluded.

Somewhere in the shrubbery, beyond the verandah steps, a lone cicada was chirring, whilst further afield towards the river a bull gave a melancholy bellow. Margaret pushed the sheet further off her shoulder. How hot it was, she thought. It was a long time before she finally fell asleep. Her mind seemed full to bursting with the experiences and anxieties of the past two weeks.

"Wake up Marge. Come on, wake up. It's breakfast time." Alice pleaded as she gently shook her friend by the shoulder. Margaret stirred

"Oh Heavens!" she yawned.

"Whatever time is it? It can't be five o'clock already, I feel as if I've only just gone to sleep." she groaned as she reluctantly discarded her sheet and climbed off the creaking iron bed.

Pushing back the canvas curtain that had so alarmed her during the night she peered out into the homestead garden. Already it was broad daylight, although the sun still hung low in the Eastern sky, throwing long cool shadows across the damp lawn.

The air felt deliciously cool after the hot breathless night and was filled with the songs of unfamiliar birds. Friar and miner birds hung suspended in the gum trees, feeding upon the nectar of the feathery blossom, whilst finches picked at invisible morsels amongst the grass beneath.

Beyond the corner of the main building an elderly Aboriginal woman was aimlessly watering shrubs, her hose throwing a fine silvery spray onto the glistening foliage. A bough shed stood apart from the homestead close to which a second native woman was raking fallen leaves beneath a frangipani tree.

The two girls, having washed, dressed and pinned up their hair, made their way into the dining room adjoining the verandah where they had slept. It was a little past five o'clock when they took their seats, but they were not sufficiently late to incur any undue criticism. Their host, Ted Millard, appeared to be a most amiable person taking upon himself the role of father figure to the two young nursing sisters who had travelled so far from their own families for the benefit of the local inhabitants.

The lack of any medical assistance in the area had long been a source of grave concern to the pastoralists and residents of Fitzroy Crossing. There had been many unnecessary losses of life, including one of Ted Millard's predecessors, George Poole, who had died of appendicitis at an early age. He was only one of many, but it was his popularity and lost potential that made his case seem particularly tragic. Now these two brave young women had come to ease the burden of responsibility in times of sickness. What a blessing they would be if they proved able to meet the task in front of them.

It was perhaps just as well that the hospital building was not quite complete, Ted thought as he watched his two young charges pick their way delicately through the large slabs of steak served to them. A day or two out at Go Go would give them time to adjust a little to the climate and lifestyle of the Kimberley before they plunged headlong into the task ahead.

Having done their best to do justice to the grotesquely large meal, Alice and Margaret returned to their verandah room to tidy the beds and collect their hats. They were embarrassed to find the covers already tucked and straightened and resolved to tidy their room before breakfast in future.

A skinny legged, native girl was brushing the footpath as they left the building. A large canvas water bag hung on the verandah. Margaret eyed it with distaste. Another communal drinking supply, she supposed. Doubting the cleanliness of the container she emptied it onto the grass and re-filled it with clean water, meaning to make this a daily task. She felt cleanliness and hygiene were the key to good health and it was her mission to ensure that she did what she could to promote it. It was some days later that Mr Millard came across her as she performed this self appointed task.

"You know Margaret" he told her kindly,

"I empty and re-fill that water bag every evening, so that the water has a chance to cool overnight." Margaret, looking up from the tap, blushed with embarrassment. How foolish he must think her. Daily she had been carefully throwing out the cool water and replacing it with warm tap water. He must think her a trying guest indeed. She apologized for her mistake and determined to be a little less interfering in future.

One morning Ted Millard offered to take them for 'a run' after breakfast to look at the station. 'A run' Margaret thankfully reasoned meant 'a drive', for in this heat anything more energetic seemed quite out of the question. Used as she was to the scenery of New England, with its green undulating hills and pretty valleys, Go Go Station seemed to Margaret very sparse indeed. How such a desolate landscape was able to sustain any form of life seemed a great puzzle to her. That GoGo, said to be a fine cattle property, could carry a herd of such numbers as Mr. Millard supposed, seemed to her the height of improbability.

She was interested to see, later in the morning, a mob of cattle, several hundred strong, camped alongside one of the station's man-made watering points. A deep reddish brown, the animals lay chewing their cud in the dusty shade of bauhinia trees. Their frames, though large, were thin and bony, and about their eyes pink hairless circles gave them a peculiar bespectacled appearance.

"Those rings are caused by the flies" Mr. Millard told the girls at their enquiry, adding

"It's a bad time just now for cattle. Not much feed and all the natural waters dried up, but they'll pick up when the wet comes. This country really blooms then, just wait till you see it." And he went on over endless miles of dry, dusty tracks recounting the incomparable joys of the "Wet".

Alice and Margaret remained guests at GoGo for several days, enjoying the kindness of their host and the lush coolness of the well watered grounds. They slowly became accustomed to the heat and humidity that seemed only to abate at dawn when they were obliged to rise. As the weariness of their journey left them and their natural good spirits returned they began eagerly to await news of the hospital's completion.

CHAPTER SEVEN

The A.I.M Hospital

1939 – 1941

Ben Hargraves, the builder, was camped in a large tent. It was overgrown with passionfruit vines and anyone looking at it from a distance might easily have mistaken it for a bough shed. Preferring to do all of the building himself, his cool vine clad tent served not only as a temporary home, but also as his workshop. He had built many A.I.M. hospitals over the years in various localities, but for the heat of Fitzroy Crossing he found his modest dwelling comfortable and practical enough to meet his needs.

Hearing of the arrival of the two nursing sisters from New South Wales, Ben Hargraves had been working tirelessly to complete the new building. It was now almost the end of October and the oppressive heat of the previous few days heralded the onset of the first early storms. The 'Wet' season was fast approaching. Ben Hargraves was well aware of the urgency to complete his task. He worked on what he saw as the more essential aspects of the hospital building. Once these were completed to his satisfaction he arranged for Padre Chris Goy to deliver and install a small Delco lighting plant that was to serve as the power supply for the hospital. As soon as this was done a message was sent to the two nurses at GoGo that the hospital was now ready to be occupied. With mixed emotions Margaret and Alice moved from GoGo into town.

***Ben Hargraves working outside the new
A.I.M. Hospital at Fitzroy Crossing. 1939***

Alice, being senior by three years, was the natural leader. She had lost her mother at the age of ten. Since then she had had various homes that made her seem to Margaret older than her years, and it was to Alice that she looked for guidance and reassurance in the earliest days of their mission to Fitzroy Crossing.

"Alice have you been out to see the toilet?" Margaret whispered as she met her friend coming down the stairway of the new building.

"Not yet, why?" Alice replied.

"It hasn't got a bucket in it!" Margaret said, her face a study of indignation.

"Then we'll have to find one and make do" Alice told her shortly.

"What do you think of the place otherwise?" she asked in a kinder manner.

"It looks reasonable enough to me."

Margaret looked about her. It was a large two storey building, constructed mainly of timber and iron. At ground level glass double doors led into a spacious room with a concrete floor. There was a small cooking area at one end in which stood a wood stove. A timber stairway led to the upper part of the building where two patients could be accommodated. A small enclosed dressing room was situated to one side, with rather cramped sleeping quarters for the nursing staff at the further end of the room. Large iron shutters provided the only means of ventilation at both levels and being a windless day the whole building felt stiflingly hot.

The A.I.M hospital kitchen with a wood stove, cold water tap and kerosene tin. Circa 1939.

The A.I.M. hospital in October 1939, before a tank was on the stand or the garden was started.

Outside and a little apart from the hospital building were two smaller constructions. One consisting of a laundry and shower, the other a tiny tin shed containing the incomplete bucket toilet that offended Margaret. A chimney stack for the wood stove and a tank stand, still without a rainwater tank, were located at the kitchen end of the building. Beyond it was the builder's well disguised tent.

Apart from the passion vine there was no vegetation of any description, the whole area being covered in hot fine sand. Margaret, still smarting from Alice's earlier retort concerning their sanitation arrangements, was reluctant to find further fault. Ignoring the other obvious shortcomings such as the unfinished tank stand she chose instead to agree that the place would more than suffice.

"Of course Mr. Hargraves still has some finishing off to do" Alice remarked as they looked at the general clutter of timber off cuts, wood shavings and the occasional bent nail that littered the concrete floor.

"Come on Margaret, let's set to and get ourselves unpacked and sorted out a bit." she added, briskly walking across to where a number of boxes lay stacked against the end wall.

The two young women spent a busy day settling in. They swept and cleaned, dusted and hosed until the building finally satisfied them. Then they sorted through the many packages sent on ahead of them from Sydney, until they discovered the bed linen. Beds were made, cases unpacked and medical provisions put carefully away. Several times during the afternoon their work was interrupted by the arrival of would be patients. None of these people appeared to be suffering from any undue ills, other than perhaps chronic curiosity, and apart from hindering the girls progress caused them no great concern. The heat, however, was another matter. Perspiration glistened on their flushed faces and uncomfortably damp clothing clung wetly across their tired shoulders.

Not until the sun had gone down, leaving the sky a magnificent study of orange and gold did the two young women cease work. Taking long drinks of cold water from their kerosene refrigerator they went outside to sit and talk with Ben Hargraves near his tent. It had been a long and exhausting day, but a sense of achievement and satisfaction helped relieve their tiredness, feeling that they were now reasonably well prepared for whatever tomorrow might bring.

◆ ◆ ◆

It took Sisters Alice Hall and Margaret Coakes some while to adapt to their new situation. They quickly discovered that the routine process of cleaning and unpacking was relatively straight forward compared to other adjustments that had to be made.

Initially they had been determined to wear their full nursing uniforms, complete with stockings and veils Wishing to maintain their high standards they at first endured this discomfort, but soon found their veils an unnecessary encumbrance, brushing as they did against Ben's wet paintwork. These were discarded and shortly after the stockings also were abandoned.

The matter of sleeping arrangements was a cause of concern for Margaret, who wished to sleep within the safe confines of their hot airless bedrooms. When sleep was found to be impossible there Alice suggested that they should shift the beds outside and sleep beneath the stars, their only protection being mosquito nets. A good night's sleep was clearly of great importance for people working as hard as she and Alice. After consulting their newly found friend Ted Millard, Margaret reluctantly agreed to this arrangement.

"Do you really think it is safe?" Margaret had asked shyly. "It is so much cooler outdoors, but we don't want to be bothered by anyone."

"No-one will dare to trouble you girls" He assured her. "If they did they would likely be lynched"

As added security, the manager of GoGo arranged for two of the station natives, a married couple called Hansen and Jumbung, to move into town to look after the young women. As well as keeping an eye on the girls they assisted at the hospital with the daily chores of watering, bread making and cleaning. Alice and Margaret became particularly fond of Jumbung, or Jum as she was affectionately known, who soon became not only companion, helper and friend, but later even acted as chaperone.

Mr. Millard's assistance continued with the donation of a large figwood table and later the erection of a fence around the perimeter of the hospital. A long bough shed, that would become additional accommodation for native patients, was also built by some of his station hands. As chairman of the Australian Inland Mission in Fitzroy Crossing he was deemed to be the right person to have the honour of formally opening this new hospital.

The opening of the
A.I.M. Hospital. November 8th 1939.

Back Row L-R. Rev. Ray Nobe. (Methodist Minister),
Rev. Chris Goy (Presbyterian Minister), Dr. Sweetman,
(Wyndham), Constable Steve Tully, Bert Dunn.

Front Row. Sr Alice Hall, Pilot Robinson, Sr. Margaret Coakes,
George Congrieve (plane mechanic).

The A.I.M Hospital

The ceremony took place on November 8th, 1939. There was a good attendance at the opening, despite a recent heavy thunderstorm that prevented several of the nearby station folk from making the journey into town. Within a matter of days the two patient beds upstairs were occupied.

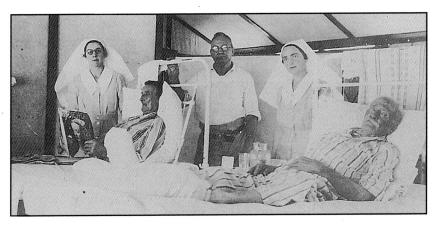

The hospital's first two patients. L-R. Sr. Coakes, Bill Smidt (GoGo Blacksmith), Ted Millard (Manager of GoGo station), Sr. Hall and Bill Mack.

The first new patient, suffering from arthritic hands, was a blacksmith called Bill Smidt, the other was eighty four year old Bill Mack. Bill Mack had dry gangrene in one leg. He did not want to be transferred to Derby, preferring to remain where he was to die at Fitzroy Crossing. This he did some two months later.

They buried him the same day. His body, stitched up in canvas and supported by two shovel handles, was gently lowered into the ground by garden hose, in place of rope. Alice Hall read the funeral service. Many of the townspeople attended, the men dressed in new white shirts bought for the occasion. After the ceremony the gathering adjourned to the hotel for refreshments. Alice and Margaret, both of whom abhorred any form of alcohol, sat in the hotel garden drinking lemonade.

"It seemed odd having no coffin for him" Margaret remarked as she sipped her cool drink

"And all done within a day of his passing" she mused absent-mindedly.

"Well that's the heat Margaret" Alice reminded her.

"There's nowhere to keep him, and really what's the point of delaying. Still I'm glad all those people turned up for the service. He must have been well thought of round here don't you think?"

"Either that, or they like a good wake" Margaret smiled wryly.

"Still I'll miss him won't you? All that calling out for ice night and day. We must let GoGo and Fossil Downs know we don't need them to bring it anymore." The nature of the old man's illness had called for copious quantities of ice, more by far than their little kerosene refrigerator was able to produce. The nurses had requested anyone who was passing by the hospital to bring a billy can of ice with them from the hotel.

With patients already in residence and numerous others attending their clinic Alice and Margaret had devised a roster system to share the workload. One would do the cooking and domestic chores whilst the other attended to the nursing duties, changing week and week about.

The hospital soon became not only a much needed medical outpost but also a popular social gathering place. As part of their duties with the Australian Inland Mission the nursing sisters were encouraged to provide a congenial meeting place for local inhabitants. In this way they endeavoured to provide an alternative to excessive hours of drinking at the hotel.

A gramaphone had been donated by A.I.M. supporters and a piano was brought in from Noonkenbah by Campbell Dempster. These were installed in the large downstairs room that was converted into a general social meeting area. People were encouraged to come to read, sing or listen to music. Alice sometimes played the piano and impromptu sing-a-longs often resulted.

Needless to say the hotel proprietor, Dick Fallon, was not altogether pleased by this development, luring as it did his patrons away from his licensed bar. It was now made easy for young men, including those who had assembled on the dirt airstrip on the day of Margaret and Alice's arrival, to become acquainted with the nurses. Sam Thomas and George Wells were regular visitors, the latter even going so far as to bring the girls gifts in the form of bottled cool drink and even some live fowls.

"And what do you suppose we are to do with these?" Margaret reproached him the day he delivered the hens.

"As if there isn't enough for us to do here without minding a mob of scratching chooks!"

George Wells, manager of Cherrabun Station, was a tall dark haired man. Balding somewhat and fast approaching forty he was still a bachelor. Having lived nearly all his life at Fitzroy Crossing where white women were few, and single women as rare as hens teeth, he could not help but be drawn to the two new arrivals in town. He grinned broadly at Margaret's ingratitude.

"They lay eggs" he drawled laconically. So the hens were added to the ever lengthening list of dependant beings. They roosted on top of the bough shed at night and were fed on hospital scraps by day.

As time went by Margaret and Alice's days became increasingly busy. They rose at six, sometimes having been up much of the night with sick patients. They prepared and served breakfast for everyone before calling up the Flying Doctor on the pedal radio. They baked their own bread and attended to callers and outpatients.

They had few medical supplies. Such items as cough mixtures, eye water, sody sals for rheumatic pain, morphine tablets and disprin being the sum total of their aids against suffering. Apart from a small sterilizer they had very little medical equipment, not even a stethoscope. Bandages were made from torn calico and operating equipment was brought by the Flying Doctor when he visited.

Nursing duties included such things as suturing and tooth extractions, the latter having been learnt during a brief training session at Prince Alfred Hospital in Sydney. For this procedure patients would receive an injection of local anaesthetic. Front teeth were screwed, back teeth rocked to and forth until the offending tooth fell free. A bottle of brandy stood behind the door for the faint hearted.

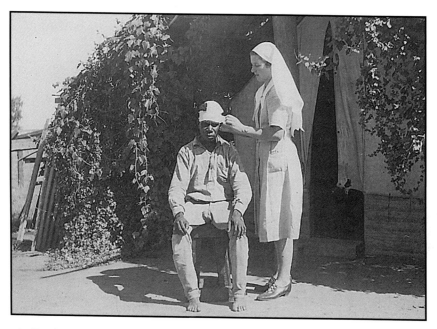

Patient 'Fred' having his dressing done by Sister Margaret Coakes outside the vine covered tent left by the builder.

As time went by and word spread of the work being done by the A.I.M. sisters at their little welfare centre come hospital, their clientele gradually increased. It was some time before the Aboriginal population became accustomed to receiving care and medical attention from the white women. Jumbung and Hansens presence helped alleviate the native's fears. The large bough shed, furnished with wooden seats and cowhide stretcher beds, proved invaluable as additional accommodation for the indigenous population, as well as acting as a waiting room when not otherwise in use during the Flying Doctor's visits. It was less intimidating to the natives and enabled the girls to cater to their needs more easily.

L-R. Fred (patient), Hansen, Jumbung and other native patients outside the bough shed at the A.I.M. Hospital. Feb. 1940.

The Flying Doctor made regular monthly visits but was otherwise only called to attend emergencies, as happened when a twelve year old white boy was brought in with severe abdominal pain. Leaving Margaret with the sick child and his father, Alice got on the pedal radio to the doctor at Wyndham. Detailing the symptoms, appendicitis was diagnosed. Arrangements were made for the doctor to fly down to Fitzroy Crossing that afternoon. He would bring with him his theatre sister and the necessary sterilized operating equipment in sealed drums. Alice, seated at the pedal radio in the mid-day heat, found communication difficult. As she tried to decipher the doctor's message through the static, a little pool of perspiration slowly spread on the concrete floor at her feet from the exertion of pedalling.

It was dusk before the plane landed. On board was the doctor, theatre sister, mechanic, radio operator and the pilot Cyril Kleinig, with their equipment. The young patient, Stewart Orr, was placed on the kitchen table where Margaret administered the open ether anaesthetic. The doctor instructed her to keep the patient's chin up and ensure that he did not swallow his tongue.

Meanwhile the boy's father waited downstairs with a lantern, whilst the radio operator stood close at hand with a three cell torch and spare batteries, in case the uncertain power supply failed. The operation was carried out successfully beneath a single sixty watt light globe.

Alice and Margaret, exhausted from the events of the day, were obliged to feed and accommodate the visitors, who departed early the following morning. Left with their young patient and instructions to remove the stitches in ten to twelve days they thankfully set about the task of nursing him back to good health. He died some forty five years later at the age of fifty seven.

The problem of communication with the outside world was considerable. Apart from their daily sched. with the base at Wyndham, they relied on the pedal radio set for much advice and assistance when difficult cases presented at the hospital. Pedalling and talking on the antiquated piece of apparatus was strenuous and exhausting and atmospheric conditions frequently made contact unreliable. There were only three telephones in the area, these being at the Post Office, the Hotel and GoGo Station.

On one occasion when transmission proved impossible, Margaret had to walk a considerable distance, in extreme heat, to the Post Office in order to contact the doctor concerning a patient in severe pain. Before leaving him she had administered one sixth of morphine to give him some relief during her absence.

Fitzroy Crossing was situated on the banks of the Fitzroy River, which floods regularly during the monsoon. It was made up of three main groups of buildings each erected on high ground and frequently being separated from each other by floodwaters during the 'wet season. There was one hotel in the town, known as the Crossing Inn, with a general store adjacent to it. Dick Fallon was the hotel proprietor and Arthur Gardiner the store-keeper. The latter also maintained a good vegetable garden that flourished on the rich river silt and provided a supply of fresh produce to the local inhabitants.

Dick Fallon was not altogether in favour of the nurses' influence in the town and terms between the hospital and hotel were slightly strained. Margaret did not feel she could impose on the publican for the use of his telephone, choosing instead to make use of the service provided at the Post Office where the postmaster and linesman each had a cottage.

The nearest dwelling to the A.I.M. hospital was the Police Station which lay across the Brooking Creek. Situated close-by was a goat yard belonging to the police who provided the hospital with fresh goats milk daily. Having a vehicle, the police frequently provided transport for the two nurses, taking them up to the store for supplies and across to the post office if they had mail to send.

On the day in question there was no lift available for Margaret at the Police Station and she trudged through the heat and along the dusty tracks to the Post Office alone. She was flushed and soaked with perspiration when she arrived, but anxiety for her patient, rather than exhaustion, was uppermost in her mind as she called up the doctor for advice. She was astounded to hear herself being severely rebuked when she informed the doctor that pain relief had already been given.

"You had no business to do that" he had chided, "It will conceal the man's symptoms and hinder diagnosis"

Margaret endeavouring to keep her irritation in check replied,

"We have no doctor here to consult and this patient is in extreme pain. I do not know whether it is gallstones or heart or some other cause. Whatever it may be the man is in great pain and he needs some relief!"

After further criticism Margaret was able to convince the doctor that her patient should be transferred to Derby Hospital. It was a two day journey, overland, between the two towns. The road followed the river and there were more than two dozen gates to open along the route, so patients were necessarily airlifted out.

Margaret was relieved no longer to be burdened by the man's extreme suffering. Only a matter of days later she heard that her patient, evidently not getting sufficient pain relief in Derby after all, went out on the marsh and cut his own throat.

Margaret was discovering that nursing in the outback was not at all the same as hospital nursing. Left to her own devices she relied heavily on common sense and improvisation. She discarded many of the less practical procedures adopted in city hospitals and, apart from maintaining scrupulous personal hygiene, devoted most of her endeavours to ensuring her patients were kept comfortable. She did not feel bound by strict rules and authoritarian matrons. When she was confronted with the problem of Junkabine her handling of it was more practical.

Junkabine was a grey haired Aboriginal man from Christmas Creek Station, who had once been a police tracker. On arrival at the Fitzroy Crossing Hospital he had a high fever, chest pain and grunting respiration, from which Margaret diagnosed pneumonia.

She took her new patient across to the vine clad tent, left by the builder, and put him to bed. He was wearing six shirts, but despite the severity of his condition he was still able adamantly to refuse to have any of them removed. He was equally vehement when Margaret endeavoured to wash him.

Standing in the canvas shelter, optimistically holding a basin of warm soapy water, Margaret recalled a similar occasion during her training days when she had encountered a patient who refused to be washed. He had been an unfortunate homeless derelict, brought to the Marrickville Hospital feeling unwell. Margaret was instructed to wash him.

"Please don't wash me nurse." the man had pleaded.

"If you do I will surely die. I haven't had a wash for years." Margaret had looked at him sympathetically.

"If I could I would just cover you up and give you your medicine" she had told him.

"but it is more than my job is worth to disobey my orders." and she firmly removed his clothes and scrubbed him down with monkey soap. The man died twenty-four hours later. The fact that he was clean was of little consolation to the trainee nurse who so many years later still remembered his plea.

Now gazing down at the Aboriginal man, Junkabine, Margaret was thankful that she was solely responsible for his care. She had no matron to whom she need justify her actions, but was able to concentrate instead on her single minded task of making him well. She did not insist on taking off his numerous shirts and discarded her soap and water. Instead she plied him with fluids and cough mixture.

In the early hours of the morning, when she heard him groaning and coughing, she lit the lantern and crossed to his bed where she administered a sixth of morphine. This she did by dissolving a tablet in a teaspoon of previously boiled water and drawing it up in a syringe. With great difficulty she rolled up the six shirt sleeves to give the injection. This became a nightly practice.

The sound of Margaret's nocturnal visits to her elderly patient caused some disturbance in the precincts of the hospital, for seeing the lantern swinging, and hearing her shuffling step across the dusty ground George Wells' rooster would invariably start crowing and set the remaining fowls squawking with alarm. However, her patient gradually recovered until one morning she found his bed empty.

"Where have you been?" she asked when he returned a good while later.

"For a walk, to make my legs strong" he had told her.

It was to be many months and greatly altered circumstances before they met again.

Life at the little hospital, apart from being hard work, was rewarding in many ways. With the assistance of their Aboriginal helpers, Hansen and Jumbung, they gradually got a modest garden established that greatly alleviated the problem of dust blowing through the building, as well as enhancing the outlook. They were able to provide eggs for themselves and their patients, fresh milk from the police station and vegetables, courtesy of Arthur Gardiner's store. They also built up quite a reasonable collection of plain but serviceable furniture, much of it made from old timber packing cases. Small stools and tables made from kerosene packaging, beds of wood and woven strips of cattle hide and the large native fig table donated by GoGo.

They had a pair of Mrs. Potts flat irons with which to iron the linen tray cloths and their own starched uniforms, so that they were able to maintain the hospital in a clean, comfortable and serviceable manner. They adapted quickly to their altered circumstances and adjusted their nursing techniques accordingly. They had the added satisfaction of nursing many difficult patients back to good health.

On the social side their lives were less fulfilling, there never being an occasion when both friends were able to leave the hospital together. However the small meeting room on the ground floor, with its wind-up gramophone, books and old piano was a popular gathering place and many an enjoyable hour was spent there.

Occasionally the girls were invited out to visit one of the neighbouring stations, or simply taken for a short drive within the precincts of the tiny outback town.

Both Alice and Margaret were greatly admired, not only for their fortitude and professionalism, but also amongst the male population for their obvious good looks and attractive personalities. Neither were lacking in attention from the opposite sex, in spite of the fact they never consciously encouraged it. Indeed Margaret positively shunned it, insisting on one occasion, when a lengthy drive out to Oscar Range Station was necessary to evacuate Mrs. Bletchington, that Jumbung accompany her to act as a chaperone. Her prudery caused some amusement in the district.

On another occasion Margaret had been outraged to learn of a proposed local appeal to be mounted on their behalf. Never having seen women in uniform, someone had noted that the girls only seemed to own one dress. Margaret was not one for accepting gifts from anyone, far less if it smacked even slightly of charity. She was a generous giver, but graceful acceptance was not in her nature, as even her most stalwart admirers were soon to discover.

One persistent admirer was the manager of Cherrabun Station. George Wells, already forty and still single, frequently made the two hour journey into Fitzroy Crossing. Combining station business with a pleasurable visit to the new hospital, he was already well known for his generosity and kindness. Indeed the fowls that roosted on top of the bough shed that provided a constant supply of fresh eggs for the hospital had been the first of many presents to the sisters. Shunned by Margaret at the time, she now had to own that 'the mob of scratching chooks' did have their uses. But when George presented her with a dog called Pepper she refused his gift point blank.

"And don't tell me this thing will serve any good purpose" she had scolded. "You can take it away, for I, sure as anything, don't want it."

"Oh Margaret! " exclaimed Alice indignantly,

"How can you say such a thing. It's adorable, and if you haven't the grace to accept Pepper then I will." and with that George had presented his gift to Alice instead.

He did however manage to make some headway with Margaret over the following months. He quite often brought bottles of cool drinks for both her and Alice, and would take whichever of them was free at the time, for short drives about the place.

Margaret by this time had learned to curb her previous unreasonable distrust of all males. She had gained greatly in self confidence and experience. Frequently having to deal with difficult and tiresome patients she unconsciously acquired such a knowledge of peoples' personalities that she soon found herself able to assess their character. She felt, instinctively, that George was more 'on the level' than most men. He had always been straight and honest with them and he did not irritate her with needless small talk, malicious gossip or unpleasant rough language.

He was a good looking man, tall and strongly built, slightly bald with dark hair and fine features. He was immensely strong, fit and agile. Margaret had first been impressed by his agility when, encountering difficulties with the radio, he had shinned up the precariously high slender post unassisted to attend to the problem of the aerial for them.

*2nd from left. Billy Wells. Far right, George Wells aged 20.
Taken at Brooking Springs station Oct. 1920.*

Born in Adavale, Queensland in 1900, he had first come to the
Kimberley with his mother and sister, Nora, at the age of four. Hunted
out of the Gulf Country by the drought, they had re-joined his father
Billy Wells, growing up on the Oscar and Brooking Springs Stations
which his father was then managing for the Blythes.

Billy Wells, in his seventies, was still working in the Kimberley,
mostly as camp cook for droving teams, during the cattle season.
George's mother, Martha, lived in Perth. She had borne her husband
six children during the course of their marriage, two of whom had
died at Brooking Springs. The first, a daughter, Freda, aged three
and four years later a son James Clinton, aged two. George Poole,
formerley manager of GoGo, was a brother of Martha's and the only
direct family she had on this side of the continent. When he was
struck down with appendicitis during the "wet" of 1924 the overland
evacuation to Derby had been lengthy. Many flooded creeks had to
be negotiated and he contracted peritonitis before arriving, finally,
in Fremantle. With his death Martha felt the Kimberley had cost her
dearly and left for Perth that year, never to return.

Billy Wells continued to seek seasonal employment in the Kimberley until he was well advanced in years. He was a good deal shorter than his son George, straight and thin with white hair that showed no trace of having been ginger in his youth.

In the wet season of 1940 Billy Wells was brought in to the A.I.M. hospital with symptoms consistent with pneumonia. Margaret was on nursing duty. When he seemed not to respond to treatment and taking his age into consideration she decided it prudent to evacuate him to the Wyndham Base Hospital.

George was away on holiday visiting his mother in Perth. The rains had come and the Brooking Creek, which separated the hospital from the hotel was impassable. Margaret, who was to escort Billy to Wyndham, made arrangements to ferry her patient by boat up the flooded Fitzroy River to the hotel. From there a car was able to take them on to the small airstrip and so enable them to fly out to Wyndham.

Billie's condition continued to deteriorate. Margaret, who had remained in Wyndham awaiting a return flight, contacted George Wells advising him to visit his father before returning to Fitzroy. George needed no more encouragement than to know that Margaret was still in the small northern port town. He readily agreed to make the necessary detour. The old man, still failing to improve, was prepared for transfer to Royal Perth Hospital.

"Thank you for all you've done for me Sister Coakes" Billy said to Margaret before going. "You've been most kind."

"It was nothing" Margaret told him "And please, just call me Margaret."

"And you can call me Dad" he had responded with a twinkle in his eye. It was a remark she was to remember long after he had gone.

William Joseph Wells, known to most as Billy, was diagnosed as having cancer of the spine. He died in Royal Perth Hospital in October 1941 aged seventy four.

Billy Wells (patient) being taken down the river to catch a plane from Fitzroy to Wyndham Base Hospital.

L-R. Bill Green, Sr. Coakes, Billy Wells, Bill Mason and native helper Jumbung in the background.

CHAPTER EIGHT

A Betrothal

1941 - 1942

Vick Jones, relief manager of Christmas Creek Station, pulled up outside the A.I.M. building and strode along the footpath to the front entrance. It was an hour after sundown and the evening was sultry and still.

"Hello there! Is anyone around" he called loudly. Alice, alone in the building except for her patient upstairs, hurried from the kitchen.

"Hello Vick. How can I help you?" she asked.

"I'm wondering if you girls have seen George Wells" he said coming to the point with surprising directness. "I hear he's in town this 'arvo."

"No" replied Alice

"I don't know where he might be."

"Well maybe Margaret knows" the manager of Christmas Creek went on.

"Is she here?"

"Not at the moment" said Alice, objecting to the man's questioning, but being careful not to show it.

She had been endeavouring to keep George and Margaret's courtship a secret for several weeks. George seemed at last to be making some headway with her reluctant colleague, but Alice knew Margaret too well to believe an engagement was inevitable. The girl from Guyra needed more time. She still bore the scars of her parent's broken marriage and seemed determined to remain a spinster. George would need much patience and Alice had no intention of allowing the prattling tongues of Fitzroy Crossing to scare Margaret from her romance.

On this particular evening George, as usual, had taken her for a short drive across the flat towards the river. There, Alice knew, they would sit and talk for an hour or more before coming back for a hot drink. Should any assistance be needed at the hospital during their absence, it was arranged that a lantern would be hung out as a sign for Margaret to hurry back.

"So where is Margaret now?" Vick Jones persisted, boldly stepping past Alice.

"She is on an errand" Alice said coldly.

"An errand eh?" Vick grinned.

"Is that how it is? Well you see that hat on the piano there Alice?" he said, pointing to the far side of the room.

"looks an awful lot like George's hat to me" and he turned on his heel and left, grinning smugly.

On June 8th 1941, Margaret Coakes, aged twenty six, became engaged to George Wells, some fifteen years her senior. The proposal had been neither romantic nor memorable. It was more a result of George's persistence in wearing down Margaret's former resolve to remain single.

"What would I be wanting to get married for?" she had asked.

"I am quite all right as I am and besides, after my two years here and when the war is over, I intend to travel the world." There was a long pause. George looked at her affectionately but said nothing.

"And what if we have rows" she continued on a more promising note.

A Betrothal

"I won't be staying with you if we have rows"

"There won't be any rows" George retorted

"I promise you there won't be any rows"

He had sat placidly looking at her outraged expression. It was one of his most aggravating habits, to say nothing, but to look as if he was thinking plenty. She longed for him to put his thoughts into words so that she might respond, but he rarely did.

"I think you had better arrange with Alice to take a day off to come out and look at Cherrabun Station" he told her in a tone that indicated he thought the matter was now settled.

"If you think you can live there I'll write to Emanuel Brothers and ask if they'll agree to our marriage."

"And what if I don't think Cherrabun will suit me?" Margaret asked

"Then there'll be no point in us going any further" he responded with brutal finality.

The tall dark man beside her, seemingly so dependable and devoted, not only told Margaret bluntly to accept conditions on Cherrabun or he'd do without her, but also that he needed the boss' permission to marry. It seemed to her that the Emanuels had a far greater pull on George than she herself had. She wasn't sure that this pleased her.

"Why do you have to ask for permission to marry from your employer" she said scathingly,

"They don't even know me."

"Well I've worked for them for a long time. Six years droving and another seven running Cherrabun Station. They once refused my uncle George Poole permission to marry a lady doctor, but I have to ask them. Like it or not, that's how it is Margaret!" In his quiet voice she detected a tone of absolute loyalty and realising further protest was pointless agreed to visit Cherrabun with him the following week.

♦ ♦ ♦

Upon her engagement Margaret had written to the Australian Inland Mission giving notice of her intention to resign at the end of her two year contract, which was due to expire in October of that year. When a reply came from the organization asking her to relinquish her position as early as July, she was quite reasonably indignant. When she protested, it was explained to her that she was entitled to two months holiday and that her replacement, Sister Muriel Hatfield, would be far less troubled by the climate if she started work in July instead of coming into the intolerable heat of October.

Margaret, recalling how awful she had found the heat when she first arrived, could not object to this arrangement, even though it would put her out of work rather sooner than she had anticipated. She decided to return to her family in New South Wales for the duration of her engagement, believing that if she was to spend a lifetime in the remote West Kimberley she must now spend what time she could with her aging mother.

What George Wells must have thought of this arrangement can be well imagined. At the age of forty one, having at last found an attractive and capable lady willing to marry him, he was reluctant to see her return to her family in the Eastern States so soon after their betrothal, and must have wondered if she would ever return to him.

In July 1941 Margaret said goodbye to Alice. She packed her few belongings and boarded a small aircraft to fly to Derby, where she stayed with the Scotts, proprietors of the Club Hotel, for a few days until she was able to secure a berth on the Gorghan.

At this time the second world war was developing into a major global conflict and many people were fleeing from Singapore, which was under immediate threat from the Japanese. The Gorghan plied between Perth and Singapore and had come into the port of Derby to load a shipment of live cattle for the southern market.

With passenger accommodation in great demand Margaret was obliged to sleep in the ship's music room, there being no cabins available. It was a hot stuffy room, that smelt strongly of tobacco smoke, but the passengers sleeping there were uncomplaining. They were only too thankful to get passage to Perth. Throughout the ship was the continual stench of the wretched cattle being transported in the hold.

Because of a light left burning in the music room, Margaret found it difficult to sleep. Not wishing to make any undue fuss she decided to take care of the matter herself. She asked one of the ship's stewards to place a brown paper bag over the light to shade it. This he did and Margaret, well satisfied, was able to sleep.

Sometime later she awoke to much commotion. The other occupants of the room were all awake and talking animatedly together. There was a strong smell of burning. The light globe had evidently over heated beneath its makeshift shade, causing the paper to ignite. Apart from some alarm no great damage was done, the flames soon being extinguished.

Next morning Margaret was summoned by the ship's Captain and was accused of arson and sabotage. She found it difficult to convince him that her actions of the previous night had been thoughtless rather than malicious. The close proximity of the enemy was clearly making him edgy.

Once in Perth, at the conclusion of the voyage, Margaret stayed with her future mother-in-law Martha whom she had not previously met. Martha was nursing her ailing husband, Billy Wells, at home and although sorry to find him in such sad shape Margaret was delighted to meet the white haired old man again of whom she was so fond.

He had deteriorated significantly since she had last seen him, but the gentlemanly charm, for which she remembered him, was still evident and Margaret was happy to have this short time with him to renew their friendship. She often re-called his knowing remark in Wyndham at their last meeting and was pleased that he had lived to see the truth of his assumptions. Clearly Margaret was not going to enjoy the benefit of an affectionate father-in-law for much of her marriage, for his condition was now known to be terminal, but much comfort was had from their brief acquaintance. She was further encouraged to feel she was marrying into a sound family when George's sister, Nora, whom she also met at this time, proved to be equally personable and warm towards her. All in all it was a happy interlude before she again boarded the trans contintental train that transported her, over the following days and nights, all the way to Sydney. From there it was but a day's journey back to her home town of Guyra and a heart warming reunion with her family.

George Wells and his sister Nora. Circa 1920.

The lush green hills of New England and the chill damp climate of its winter were a wonderful tonic for the heat weary woman from Western Australia. It was not long before Margaret felt rejuvenated and finding her mother in reasonable health and spirits was soon anxious to be back in the work force. When a nursing position became available at Inverell she took it, later moving down to Sydney's Crown Street Hospital, where she had done her midwifery training some two years earlier.

During her time away from Fitzroy Crossing she wrote frequent letters to George, receiving only occasional replies in return, but sufficient to allay any anxieties she may have had concerning his well being.

Early in 1942 Margaret set forth once more on the long journey back to Western Australia. She had endeavoured to make arrangements for George to meet her, either in Perth or Broome, so that they could be married before going back to Fitzroy where no minister of religion resided. The war was at last making its presence felt, even in the remoteness of the Kimberley, with a Japanese invasion now frighteningly probable. As a primary producer of essential meat supplies George Wells had been 'man-powered'. He was not allowed to leave Cherrabun Station. His contribution to the war effort was clearly defined. It was to help ensure the continuation of a vital food source and be available to assist in the event of Japanese attack.

The relatively unimportant matter of his marriage to Margaret Coakes was, by necessity of these wartime circumstances, postponed indefinitely. Margaret completed the journey North alone, arriving at Fitzroy on January 27th 1942.

CHAPTER NINE

An Outback Wedding

1942

The 'wet' of 1942 was particularly severe. The small outback town of Fitzroy Crossing was even more fragmented than usual. The swirling muddy floodwaters of the Fitzroy River made its tracks and byways impassable by all means other than boat. The town, between storms, lay steaming and sweltering in the relentless February heat.

Margaret felt fortunate to be able to fly in. Seeing the appalling condition of the normally dry dusty thoroughfares it seemed to her remarkable that the airstrip, despite being reduced in length, was still in use.

She had been amazed, whilst gazing out of the small aircraft at the landscape below, how wide the river had become. Swollen with frequent torrential downpours and fed by numerous creeks and tributaries further upstream the mighty river had burst its banks. It had spread into a wide expanse of flotsam filled, muddy water, that seemed to be seeping ever further from the main channel of the river. Flocks of white water birds, spoonbills, ibis and stilts, showed up clearly as they winged their way across the flood plain below, whilst here and there a statuesque yellow billed crane, poised motionless in the shallows and gazed intently into the endless wetness.

As soon as Margaret alighted from the plane she was at once struck by the insufferable heat. Her dress, already damp and sticking with perspiration to her back, felt crushed and uncomfortable. The wet mud of the airstrip soiled her shoes within a few paces of the plane. Mosquitos seemed to whine incessantly about her head and the air was filled with the whirr of countless cicadas and the occasional chirrup of tree frogs.

She was taken straight to the hospital to see her friend Alice, whom she found looking drawn and tired. She had been overworking and clearly was in urgent need of a rest. This seemed impossible to arrange, especially as her assistant, Muriel Hatfield was laid up in bed with rheumatic fever.

"Now, when is the wedding to be?" Alice asked Margaret as they caught up on each others news.

"There's no minister here to conduct the ceremony, not likely to be for some time if this weather keeps up"

"I don't know Alice" Margaret sighed.

"I really think I've made a foolish mistake coming back to this" and she cast a dejected look out of the hospital shutters, where another shower was just beginning. They sat in silence for a moment listening to the heavy drops falling on the tin roof. Presently Margaret, who had been sitting at the large fig table, her head cupped in her hands and perspiration glistening at her temples, sat upright. Pushing her chair back she stood up saying

"Oh well, it can't go on forever Alice. Sooner or later we'll be married and both George and I want you to be bridesmaid. I've brought a dress, purse, shoes and a neat little hat with me. I'll show you. Mum gave me half our Christmas cake to use as a wedding cake, to make it a bit more of an occasion."

Alice smiled at her friend.

"Well, well. You haven't changed a bit. Still so organised Margaret. You'll make a great station wife for George," she laughed.

"As for the half a cake, that won't be necessary. Muriel made a lovely two tier wedding cake for you before she became ill."

"Oh, how very kind of her" Margaret said.

"We'll make it a wedding to remember after all. You will be my bridesmaid won't you?"

"Of course I will. I wouldn't miss it for anything Margaret, you must know that." Alice assured her, little knowing that it was a promise she would be unable to keep.

Margaret, staying at the hotel, spent nearly two weeks, enduring the heat and humidity of Fitzroy Crossing, waiting for conditions to improve sufficiently to enable a visiting minister to fly in. Conditions at the hotel at this time were far from ideal. The kitchen, which stood apart from the guest quarters was under water and unserviceable. Fortunately the ever resourceful Arthur Gardiner had established a makeshift kitchen on the front verandah. Here he erected a heavy metal plate that had been salvaged from an old disused motor car and on this it was possible to light up a good enough open fire to cook reasonable basic meals.

The toilet, located a short distance from the main building was not entirely submerged, but Margaret was obliged to wade through water well above her knees in order to reach the small privy. Many times she wished she could sleep through the night without having to make the uncomfortable short walk out through the flooded garden, hitching her nightgown indecently high to prevent it from getting wet.

There were several guests staying at the hotel during the flood, but Margaret was the only female. Most of the native population were away on 'walkabout' at the time, although a few remained to work at the police station and the hotel. A few days before his wedding George joined Margaret at the Crossing Inn, where they were accommodated separately as guests.

On the morning of Friday the thirteenth of February 1942 word was conveyed to the engaged couple that Jimmy Woods had successfully made the flight through to Wyndham. Jimmy Woods had twice taken his little plane down the shortened muddy airstrip in an endeavour to reach Wyndham, only to be turned back by turbulent thundery conditions. At last on the day following Margaret's 27th birthday he had made it through to the northern port town where he picked up the Methodist Inland Padre, and brought him back to Fitzroy Crossing. Margaret and George thankfully prepared themselves at last for the ceremony that would make them man and wife.

George dressed in a dark blue suit, tie and silk shirt, his hair slicked down neatly, had a modest gold wedding band safely stowed in his jacket pocket. Margaret, who took rather longer to put on her wedding apparel, eventually emerged from her room neatly clad in a new short sleeved blue dress. She carried a white purse and gloves and wore matching white shoes and a small brimmed white hat.

***George and Margaret Wells after their wedding
at Fitzroy Crossing February 1942.***

An Outback Wedding

The service was to be conducted on the Post Office verandah, but with the river swollen, flooding the townsite, it was necessary for the bride and groom to make the journey from hotel to post office upstream by boat.

Gazing across the brown murky water towards the bank Margaret was surprised to note how high the water had risen. Much of the townsite was completely submerged, the main groups of buildings comprising, hotel and store, post office, police station and hospital, standing as small islands of civilisation in an otherwise endless expanse of brown muddy water. The wooden telegraph posts, that linked the town with the seemingly distant world beyond, were showing a bare three feet above the water and the majestic river gums, their ghostly white trunks submerged beneath the murky mantle, looked more like overgrown shrubs than the stately trees she knew them to be.

As the small boat pulled alongside the post office verandah, Margaret was struck with a sudden feeling of sorrow. Alice Hall, her staunch friend and colleague, was not amongst the small gathering that awaited them. Although she had been brought a message from the hospital early that morning, Margaret had nonetheless hoped that her friend might, at the last minute, be able to attend. Alice had a seriously ill patient, the native Topsy from the police station, and with Muriel still suffering from rheumatic fever had no-one to relieve her at the hospital. Alice's promise to act as bridesmaid had to be broken and Margaret was unattended and without friend or family for what is, in the lives of most young women, their most momentous occasion.

Gathered on the small timber verandah that Black Friday of 1942, were half a dozen people to witness the marriage. Apart from Reverend Ray Noble who was conducting the service, there was the pilot Captain Jimmy Woods, the Postmaster and his wife, Mr and Mrs Reiman, Dick Fallon from the hotel and Charlie Selby, the new linesman.

Margaret and George took their place, standing side by side

before the Padre. It was immensely hot and without preamble the minister commenced the brief service. Margaret wondered whether it was the heat and humidity rising from the saturated floodplain, or the realisation of the enormity of what she was doing, that made her feel light headed and faint. She felt she was swaying, as if still on the boat, but realised with some relief that it was the shifting flow of water beyond the verandah railing that gave her the sense of constant motion.

The vast expanse of open country which lies on the Western side of Fitzroy Crossing and is known as Plum Plain was, after the prolonged heavy rains, saturated and treacherous. Cattle, trying to traverse the swampy expanse of grassland to make higher ground and better feed were frequently trapped by the glutinous black soil clinging to their hooves and legs. The wretched animals, weighed down heavily by the merciless mud, frequently died of exhaustion in the bog.

From the small aircraft, as they came in to land that morning, Jimmy Woods and the Padre saw several beasts in distress and naturally went to the creatures' aid. Dressed in their customary shorts, shoes and long socks the two men pulled them from the bog at the edge of the airstrip. They later arrived to attend George and Margaret's wedding, not only hot and weary from their exertions, but also rather dirty.

Directly in front of Margaret stood the minister. She looked down at his feet in an endeavour to cut out the view of the flood and so lessen her giddiness. She was surprised to see his socks and boots caked in mud, although George had told her what the two men had done for the unfortunate stock upon landing. She forgot her sense of unease and looked up at George beside her to see if he'd also noticed. How tall and straight he was, she thought. He looked very fine in his blue suit, despite the firm set of his jaw and rigid expression, and she felt a sudden rush of pride and respect for this man who had persuaded her to marry him. What the future would hold for them she dare not imagine, but somehow in that moment she knew they would cope. He was a dependable, capable man and competent bushman, and despite being a good deal older than herself, was strong and immensely fit.

With the war raging in Europe, even now enveloping parts of Asia, the uncertainty of marriage seemed to Margaret of small importance. She would do her best to be a good wife, run an ordered household and endeavour to bring George around to adopting her unfailing Christain faith. With God as their guide and comfort, no hardship would be too great to bear. She suddenly realised, with a sense of remorse, that her mind had been wandering and she concentrated wholeheartedly on the words of the padre's prayer.

After the ceremony was over, the documents signed and the round of congratulations duly acknowledged, the bridal party had an informal lunch at the Post Office. Then, changing out of their attire Margaret and George went down to the airstrip to see the visiting party off.

When Dick Fallon, proprietor of the Crossing Inn, climbed on board the little plane ahead of the Padre, the pilot Jimmy Woods crossed over to the newly wed couple.

"I'm sorry about this George" he started apologetically,

"but Dick Fallon is insisting he has to fly out with me today. I'm not sure of the reason, but I'm afraid I may not be able to take off with his extra weight on this shortened runway.

Margaret remembered an occasion a year ago when Alice had flown out of the Crossing with a sick patient they were evacuating to Derby. It had been Arthur Millard, Ted's nephew, she re-called. The pilot, finding himself unable to gain enough height just after take off, had called out to Alice to throw her suitcase out of the plane. Surprised and alarmed by the pilot's urgent tone she had swiftly done as he asked. Safely airborne, she had delivered her patient to

Derby later that day, but without a stitch of clean clothing to her name, nor a toothbrush or any other personal essential.

"You mean the plane can't take off with both him and the padre?" Margaret asked, looking rather perturbed.

"That's right" Jimmy Woods nodded. Pointing towards the water-logged end of the airstrip, he explained further,

"See, I lose a bit of length there, and what with Dick's cases and that... tell you what I'll do. I'll take off and see if the plane can take the weight. If so I'll land again and pick up the Padre. If it's too dodgy, Dick Fallon will just have to stay behind, but either way I'll get the Padre out."

"I see" Margaret nodded

"Well, I'm sure you know best. We'll just wait here shall we?" she asked trustingly. She thought the publican was causing an unnecessary disturbance to their arrangements.

When the little plane took off it circled once or twice before flying away. George, Margaret and the Padre watched in disbelief as it disappeared from sight. It seemed to Margaret a pity that they would have a guest for the first few days of their marriage, but it couldn't be helped. They must make the best they could of the situation. The three went together to the hotel.

"So are you two married yet?" was the cheery greeting from the hotel patrons as they walked in.

"Yes we are," Margaret answered

"But I don't feel any different!" There was general laughter amongst the small crowd. A smile hovered about George's lips. Margaret left him to talk and went in search of their belongings. She collected a loaf of bread and a short time later the three of them made their way down to the police cottage that had been loaned to them for their honeymoon.

Apart from a few eggs, which George went in search of each day, and the loaf of bread they had brought with them, they found themselves with very little to eat during these first days, particularly with the unlooked for visitor to feed as well.

So pre-occupied had Margaret been with the difficulty of securing the services of a minister, and so confounded once the Reverend Noble had actually arrived, that she had given little thought to the more mundane matter of housekeeping for their honeymoon.

Whilst isolated in the small single room cottage adjacent to the police station Margaret had time to reflect on the events of the preceding weeks. They had, fortunately, been able to accommodate their guest in the building next door, and apart from the problem of feeding him, found he was little trouble.

The weather continued hot, steamy and damp. Time hung heavily on Margaret's hands. Usually an active woman she occupied herself writing letters to her mother and to her friend, Enid, in Sydney.

> *'We were both nicely dressed and looking quite elegant for the occasion'* she wrote; *'although it was a great pity the weather was so inclement. That kind gentlemanly man Ted Millard from GoGo, of whom you have heard me speak so often, was unable to attend due to the flood. Worst of all, Alice thinks, though I can't see for the life of me that it matters one bit, was that a reception was planned for us out at GoGo Station. Of course with no-one able to move, on account of the river being up, it was out of the question, so our wedding was, of necessity, a very quiet and modest affair.*
>
> *'Edith Reiman, the post master's wife acted as witness for me, she being the only other lady present. She remarked over lunch that Friday the thirteenth was an unfortunate date on which to be married, but I think that is nothing but stupidity. I shall take no notice of such foolish superstition. I know full well that God will watch over me and see all is well with us.*

'I had a beautiful wedding cake made for me and saved what I could to post away to people. Unfortunately the weather is so humid and damp that it is in danger of going mouldy, so I'm afraid I may not be able to do as I'd intended. 'I don't know when we will move out to Cherrabun, this depends entirely on the weather, but Mr Millard is hoping to get us out to GoGo in the next day or two, the rain permitting.

'I shall write again when I can, but do not fret if you don't hear from me for a while. You have never seen such water as is here, and the mail is quite likely to be hindered even more than usual.

I must close now and find us some lunch. George has just come in with more eggs he has found. He really is a marvel. Did I tell you, Alice looks quite wretched? I do wish she would take a holiday. I shall do my best to persuade her, but with Muriel still unwell I suppose she will have to wait a while longer.

Fond love to you Enid.

Marge.

♦ ♦ ♦

Finally the rain abated over the Fitzroy Valley and the newly married couple were taken by boat across the still swollen river to the eastern bank, where Ted Millard awaited them. From there it was a short but difficult journey out to GoGo where George and Margaret were to remain until able to proceed to the more distant Cherrabun Station.

How odd it seemed, Margaret thought, to be sleeping in the same makeshift verandah room where she and Alice had spent their first hot night in October 1939. It seemed strange to remember how different things had been then. Hot, dry and airless, surrounded by mile upon mile of parched, barren grassland. She a naïve and inexperienced young woman, unyielding in her strict moral principles. Grateful, yes, but suspicious certainly, of the kindness shown to her then by their host. Now, two and a half years later, here she lay, a married woman.

George, asleep beside her, was oblivious to the cacophony of frogs outside that kept her awake so late. There seemed to be countless millions of them. No two sounding quite alike, she tried to imagine what each might look like if only she could see where they sang. The loud hoarse bark that sounded so near must be in the pipe outside she thought. It would be large and fat and green, it's grotesque lecherous black eyes protruding from an ugly flat head. She was easily able to imagine it crouching in the darkness nearby. She had seen many such frogs since her arrival in the North, most recently squatting on the toilet seat of the flooded hotel privy during one of her night visits. There, trying to brush the creature aside it had evaded her by leaping into the toilet bowl. She had found its presence irksome as she used the facility.

Other frogs singing close by her verandah room sounded less harsh to listen to. They were the smaller light brown variety, who, when their pale throats blew up like miniature balloons, all seemed to have different messages to repeat; 'knee deep, knee deep' one was calling from the topmost corner of the room, while outside in the shrubbery another seemed to be saying 'drip drip, drip drip' with unfailing monotony. Much further afield, somewhere amongst the tall lush sedges of the gilgaes and over the now verdant green river flats came a chirruping background chorus of a multitude of other frogs, all unaware of the otherwise sleeping world.

A firefly, winking eerily in the dark room distracted Margaret from her contemplation of the frog chorus outside. She watched fascinated as the pinpoint of light moved silently from one place to another. 'Min Mins' George had called them on that previous occasion when they had watched some down by the Brooking Creek during an evening drive. Margaret had never been one to spend needless time reflecting upon the natural wonders that surrounded her, and it had not been until her association with George, who marvelled and delighted at these things, that she had first been made aware of such creatures as this. The regularity with which the firefly blinked its silent signals into the darkness was restful and soothing for the young woman lying awake so late, and it was only a short time after that her heavy eyelids closed and she finally slipped into a deep sleep.

A day or two later George left his young bride in the care of Mr and Mrs Millard at GoGo, and set off on horseback to ride out to Cherrabun. It had been sometime since he had left the station to get married and his concern for the place had been mounting daily. Explaining to Margaret that he was held solely responsible for the station he managed, even during his necessary absences, he kissed her fondly and departed.

Margaret, once again, took up her pen to write lengthy letters to her family.

> *GoGo, Fitzroy Crossing,*
> *20th February 1942.*

My Dear Vera and Bill,

> *No doubt you don't receive many letters from me. However in the near future I am afraid there will be less as it may be impossible to get mail away. At the moment we do not expect a mail plane for a month or six weeks. The road mail is ten days late now and no sign of it. The flood of course is largely responsible and the shortage of men even to run a mail.*

> *I often think of you and remember you in my prayers. You can exchange letters with Mum and it will save paper and repeating what I have already said. You have no need to worry about me, I am probably much safer than you folk.*

> *We received numerous telegrams and good wishes. Our best man Max English was unable to*

be present on account of the flood. Alice also. Partly because it was a long and difficult trip by boat and foot and she had recently had another heart attack. (patient)

George has gone down to Cherrabun on horseback and will see what the road is like and will come back for me in a couple of days.

He didn't like leaving me. We rode over from the Crossing yesterday as the roads are still boggy in places.

We were married at the Post Office and the plane was supposed to wait forty minutes for the ceremony and then take the minister, Rev. Ray Noble to Wyndham. However Mr Fallon wanted to go, so it was thought two passengers may be too heavy, although it was a two seater plane, Mr Fallon being sixteen stone. The pilot decided to go up and see how it was with Fallon in and if he could not take the two he would come down and take the minister. When he got in the air he circled several times and then flew off. We were very upset as the poor man didn't have a change of clothes or anything. The country was flooded and he couldn't leave the Crossing by pack horse or car and no prospect of plane for six weeks. He has wired for a special plane, but they can't be had for love nor money. The telegragh line between Fitzroy and Derby is down at the moment and the linesman is trying to borrow pack horses to go and fix it.

George sends his love, everyone says how happy he looks. He is very good to me. I hardly have to think for myself. I have a piece of wedding cake to send for you to distribute. It will be very small, but it is surprising how much one uses even giving to just

*a few. I haven't sent to nearly all I should and what
Muriel Hatfield cut was to be distributed among one
hundred people. She made the cake and it was a
beauty, they took a snap so I hope it turns out alright,
so that you can see it.*

*The weather has been beautiful here while the
rain and flood was on, but it is starting to warm up
again now. Am very pleased I can ride a horse, even
if I can't do other things like sewing*

*Am very proud of my wedding ring. It is plain
gold and as wide as my engagement ring.*

*The head stockman drowned two horses trying
to fix the telephone between GoGo and the Crossing.*

*George is so good, that I now find if I suggest I
would like anything, he wires for it without saying
a word to me, so I will have to be more careful.
Cheerio for now. Much love and I will write when I
can. It may even be months between letters with the
war as it is.*

Love, Margie.

*P.S. Was very pleased with my birthday and wedding
telegram, also Mums and previous ones from you all.*

As the days passed Margaret watched in vain for her husband's
return, becoming increasingly vexed over his absence. He might be
responsible for the well-being of Cherrabun and its inhabitants, but
many of them would be away on 'walkabout' she thought and surely
even the seemingly unyielding Emanuel Brothers would understand
that the newly-weds needed this time to be together.

The steamy, humid days and long restless nights did little to improve Margaret's humour and despite the hosts kindness she could not help but recall her chagrin at George's departure when she had told him firmly

'I did not come back from New England to get married, George, for you to go to Cherrabun and leave me behind here. Unless you come and fetch me pretty soon, I promise you, I shall up and depart.' Daily she wondered why he did not heed her warning and return to fetch her.

CHAPTER TEN

Cherrabun

1942 - 1943

The Christmas Creek, which flows between GoGo and Cherrabun Stations and thus into the mighty Fitzroy River, stands dry and sandy for much of the year. However, when the annual monsoons descend on the Kimberley the creek froths and bubbles with life as it drains the surrounding catchment area and carries the turbulent waters down between its steep banks on the first part of a long journey to the King Sound and, ultimately, out to sea.

Many victims have been claimed over the years by the treacherous, unpredictable currents of these northern river systems. For those who have lived much of their lives in the district, flooded creeks and crossings are treated with the greatest respect.

George, having been in the area since a young boy, knew only too well the dangers of crossing rivers in flood. He was also aware that not all horses can be relied on to swim when out of their depth. A practical man, he was careful and well versed in the matter of survival, scathing in his criticism of the foolhardy.

The relentless 'wet' of 1942, continued unabated during the course of February. The formerly parched dry ground, having surpassed its capacity for absorption, was now well saturated and blooming with an abundance of life. The cracked claypans of the dry shrunken billabongs and creeks had long since been filled and a plethora of water fowl and amphibious life forms now flourished on the replenished food sources to be found there.

The Christmas Creek, as with all the creeks in the area, was fulfilling its short lived role as a giant drain for the immediate surrounding countryside, carrying the run-off from nightly storms, with flotsam and debris, down to the main channel of the fast flowing Fitzroy river.

George dismounted on the creek bank and, wiping the perspiration from his face with the back of his hand, he assessed his chances of making a safe crossing to the far side. The water level had fallen some six inches since his last inspection, but it still ran higher than was generally acceptable for crossing over. Holding his horse's reins loosely in one hand he brushed a mosquito absent-mindedly from his face whilst he listened to the water tumbling down the creek. The air was alive with the incessant whine of cicadas, making George's ears ring, and the troublesome message that had been tormenting him for several days continued to pound in his head. The very waters of the frothing creek seemed to be repetitiously chanting Margaret's warning 'shall depart, shall depart, shall depart'.

George was nearly forty-two and knew himself fortunate to have acquired a bride such as Margaret at his age. White women were not plentiful in the hot North of Australia at this time, with many an honest, hard working man obliged to spend his days a bachelor, from necessity rather than choice. Margaret was an unusually good looking woman as well as being capable and caring. Furthermore, in the few days they had shared together since their marriage, George had been delighted by her. Certainly she showed signs of independence and rather forthright behaviour, but the more he considered this aspect of her nature the better pleased he was. She would have a difficult time as the wife of a station manager and such strength of character would surely stand her in good stead for the future that lay before them.

It was already past mid-day and storm clouds were again gathering into tumultuous, threatening warheads, billowing whitely above, but dark and heavy beneath. There would certainly be more rain before nightfall, George considered, and the creek may well have risen again by morning. If he was to reach GoGo he must take his chance now, for in all probability it would be a week or so before the water would drop again to its present level. Cautiously he coaxed his horse down the slippery embankment and seeking the most even footing headed out into the swollen creek.

There are many pitfalls that may ensnare the ill informed and unwary when negotiating a flooded waterway, the smoothest running, less turbulent parts of the river often proving the deepest and most treacherous. George picked his way carefully out into the creek, avoiding the worst of the current for as long as he was able. A certain amount of debris was being carried downstream, but because the 'wet' season was already well advanced the accumulation of dead twigs and logs from the 'dry' had long since been swept away. Suddenly the horse beneath him stumbled and momentarily lost its footing. Caught by the swift strong current George was swept away and within seconds found himself carried downstream by the strength of the water.

A younger less experienced man, finding himself jostled and tossed about as he hurtled downstream, might well have panicked and fought for control. George, however, had the benefit of a life's experience in the North. Rejecting the natural impulse to overcome the force of the current he allowed himself to be carried with it, concerning himself only with avoiding logs and other obstacles against which he might be flung.

Eventually he was swept into a long deep bend, where a paperbark tree, on the far side of the creek, hung low over the water. It's trunk and branches were festooned with trailing debris caught there when the water level had been higher. Finding himself almost becalmed George grasped a low slung branch firmly, using his powerful arms to swing himself up onto it. He sat straddled over the branch above the swollen creek shaking the water from him. He cast his eyes upstream. The current that had swept him so deftly downstream had deposited his mare a short distance away, on the same side of the creek. George was thankful to see that she appeared unharmed. She was standing, wet and dejected, with mud up to her hock.

He had been fortunate after all, he thought, as he clambered along the limb and onto the bank. He retrieved his mount and proceeded with his journey. He wanted to reach GoGo by nightfall. His clothing soon dried and by the time George at last rode up to the homestead they only showed darkly where perspiration soiled them. Margaret, thankful to see him, welcomed his return with an unusually warm show of affection. George, undemonstrative and tired from his exertions, extracted himself from her embrace saying

"Well, I came Margaret." No reference was made of his near fatal crossing of the Christmas Creek earlier that day. Not even in the privacy of their small verandah room did he mention the risk he had taken. No good could possibly come of her knowing the extent of his folly to do her bidding, he thought.

It was not until many months later that Margaret heard of the events of that day. Whether embellished or not in the telling, the story of George's swim shook her as few things were to shake her in her lifetime. Recognizing that George had taken such a risk, as a direct result of her own impatience and selfish desire to have him near her, she was made to realize how close she had come to losing her new husband. Chastened, albeit belatedly, she was to remember the incident for the remainder of her life.

As the 'wet' drew to a close and the country slowly began to dry out and become easier to traverse, Ted Millard drove his two guests from GoGo as far as the Christmas Creek. Still impassable to vehicles, the creek bore little resemblance to the frothing torrent of previous weeks. Here they bade him farewell, and crossing the creek on foot, George and Margaret clambered into the Cherrabun vehicle that had been sent out to meet them.

Cherrabun homestead was built in the old style of timber and tin with antbed floors. The floors were watered daily by two native girls with watering cans and then swept. This kept them firm and hard enough to be serviceable.

Margaret, finding herself mistress of what had hitherto been a bachelor's abode, was quick to set about putting the place in order. The dwelling had two bedrooms, a flywire dining area, the inevitable verandah and a small storeroom.

Despite the difficulties of war time, George had done his utmost to ensure that the store was well stocked. In addition to the usual supplies neatly stacked on the shelves, he had also taken the precautionary step of concealing others beneath the store-room floor boards. Such items as golden syrup, jam and tinned butter were hidden there as emergency rations, in case of the expected Japanese invasion now so much feared by Kimberley residents.

'*Have no fear*' Margaret had written home to her mother on this subject, '*if the Japs land George says we will head for the hills. He is a good bushman and 'true blue'*. It was not until many years later that Margaret appreciated the agitation such a letter must have caused her fond parent.

At about this time Margaret, believing her husband away on some errand about the station, was alarmed by the sound of a plane flying close by. Thinking this to be the start of a Japanese attack she was filled with dread. She ran to the kitchen and snatched up a warm loaf from the mornings baking and tucking it under her arm fled down to the river. She intended to hide in one of the creek gullies and was well pleased that she had thought to bring food. She was, however, pulled up short by the sudden appearance of George riding back towards the homestead. He looked down at her flushed face and the crisp fresh loaf under her arm.

"Where are you going?" he asked in some surprise.

"Down to the river to hide." She answered proudly.

"There's a plane flying round that I think must be the Japs!"

"And what about me?" he asked,

"Do I get to come too?"

She was needled into answering

"Well George, you've always told me you could look after yourself." He laughed outright at that.

"And so I can Margaret" he grinned. He dismounted and kissed her fleetingly, still smiling broadly.

"Come on home. It's not the Japs dear. I saw the plane as I was riding in" and putting an arm loosely about her waist walked her companionably back towards the homestead.

George was not given to open displays of affection, although those who knew him well were aware of his extreme sensitivity. Beneath his firm intimidating exterior there beat a heart as tender as any. He was a fair minded man, fiercely loyal and hard working, who expected, always, equal loyalty and labour from those about him. To those who did not fill this requirement he often appeared ruthless, if not brutal, and it was this side of his nature that seemed to many mostly displayed to the world. If the other inhabitants of Cherrabun Station could have seem him now, strolling along the home track, one arm loosely about Margaret's waist, the other idly holding the reins of his stockhorse they would have been profoundly surprised.

But it was not to be, for as soon as the first dwelling was in sight he dropped his arm and turned away toward the horse yard, leaving Margaret to make the last of the walk home on her own. She had a stitch in her side, and felt hot and clammy from her headlong dash to the river.

George stepped briskly onto the verandah, perplexed by the sound of a hen squawking in alarm. A snake amongst the fowls perhaps, was his passing thought, but this was quickly dispelled by the extraordinary scene before him. He stopped abruptly and standing motionless in the deep verandah shade, watched. Fowls were scattered all across the flat at the front of the homestead. Feathers ruffled and necks stretched high, stiff with fright, they strutted through the hot dust, squawking. Two native girls appeared from behind the log heap each carrying a hen held firmly by the legs. With wings flapping and necks craning upwards, the birds voiced their alarm for all the station to hear.

George continued to wait and watch.

"Bring them here Mary. Quickly" Margaret called, stepping out from the blacksmith's shop with an axe in her hand.

"I'll chop off their heads and then we'll burn them."

"Burn them Missus!!" shrieked Mary in indignation.

"We eat 'em, missus, not burn 'em."

"Oh no you won't" stated Margaret matter of factly, her face red with excitement and exertion.

"I don't want boss to see these fowls Mary. We're just tidying up, see? They've hardly got any feathers these ones and they make the place look untidy" and with this pronouncement she swung the axe swiftly down onto the wood block, severing the head from the first of the hens.

What on earth did this unpredictable bride of his think she was doing? wondered George.

Clamping his jaw firmly, he leaned his tall lean frame against the timber post. Both hens were now decapitated. Watched reluctantly by the dusky housegirls Margaret tossed them onto a waiting fire to burn. The three women then proceeded to stalk the remaining fowls, presently capturing three more.

Soon these too, twitching and headless, were carried across to the fire. The acrid smell of burnt feathers wafted up to the verandah where George waited for his wife to finish the needless slaughter.

Margaret was hot and exhausted, but well pleased with her morning's work. What a piece of luck George had gone away for the day she thought, as she brushed her hair back from her moist brow. She stepped up the path and onto the verandah ——

"——Oh! George! I thought you were out," she exclaimed guiltily.

"So I see" he drawled in his characteristically laconic manner.

"And that's five less eggs you'll have to cook breakfast with from now on" So saying George turned on his heel and walked away, leaving Margaret wondering foolishly whether her husband was seriously annoyed.

She recalled her previous attempts to set the homestead in order. There was the time when George returned from town with his boss Ted Millard, Emanual's Manager and Pastoral Inspector from GoGo, to find that she had ruthlessly chopped down the main support in the house, badly damaging the wall in doing so. It wasn't until George had got another piece of timber wired and twitched in place that he'd explained to her the purpose of the beam. She remembered how terrified Mary had been, perched precariously on a chair on the kitchen table with axe in hand, as she cried to Margaret. 'But Missus, boss'll kill me, if I chop 'em down. He will missus!" Perhaps Mary had understood, as she did not, the damage they were doing.

***Native helpers at Cherrabun station. July 17th 1943.
L-R. Dollie, Mary and Kitty.***

Another time, soon after her arrival, she had upset George by removing his saddle, bridle and his most useful tools from the safety of their bedroom. She had felt that the tack room was the right place for them. Then she had cleared the verandah of an assortment of saddlery equipment, tackle and spare parts, loading it all into a wheelbarrow and dumping it in a breakaway at the billabong. She knew his patience had been sorely tried on that occasion. She remembered his promise that there would never be any rows between them. She admired his restraint.

There seemed to be so much that needed to be done to improve the place. Her next plan had been to create a spare room in the homestead. Cherrabun had, like most outlying stations, a large grocery store well stocked with essential food supplies. Adjacent to the main store, was a small room where boots, trousers, hats and blankets were stored. She had plans to shift these items into the main grocery store, thus creating an extra room.

Since her arrival on the station, she and George had shared their sparce two bedroomed dwelling with one of the station hands. Ted McKean had been sleeping up at the house for sometime and, apparently, neither he nor George saw any need for a change with the arrival of the new bride. Margaret felt this arrangement was an encroachment on their privacy and as Ted McKean showed a marked dislike of women in general, she wanted him away from the house. She arranged for him to be accommodated in the new vacant room next to the store, keeping the other as a spare for any visitors she might wish to have to stay. She felt sure Alice would one day come to visit her and she wanted a room ready and waiting.

Before Margaret had come to Cherrabun there had been a station cook, but he had left and so the task of feeding everyone had fallen on her own shoulders. Her days were long and hard. She rose when the grey light of dawn was barely a glimmer on the Eastern horizon to light the stove and prepare for the day ahead. She had the questionable assistance of several aboriginal women, but they were not used to working with a white woman. They disliked the 'Missus' telling them how to use the copper for boiling the clothes, overseeing the cleaning of the kitchen, the watering and sweeping of the antbed floors, the interminable business of baking bread. The boss was a hard man, but he was often away in the stock camp for days on end and not always looking over their shoulder as his wife did.

However, the food she gave out to them and their children each day was generous and wholesome, mainly stew and bread, but they wanted little more. Besides this she was soon found to be firm but efficient in dealing with the numerous ailments and mishaps that occurred in the camp amongst the piccaninies and old people. A general sense of trust and caring was presently established between them.

George was frequently absent, riding about the station run, checking waters and working in the stockcamp, sometimes for weeks on end. For Margaret the time fled. Her days were kept full and barely two hours after sundown she would collapse, exhausted, onto her bed to sleep soundly till the following dawn when the work would start all over again.

Towards the end of her first dry season on Cherrabun, Margaret found herself more tired and lethargic than ever before. She realised she was going to have a baby. George was away almost continuously, driving himself and his men hard in an effort to complete the year's mustering before the first rains.

The war was creeping ever closer as it escalated into the world's most destructive conflict. Alice Hall, who had worked herself to a state of physical and nervous exhaustion at the little AIM hospital, had at last returned to New South Wales, together with Muriel Hatfield. The small Crossing hospital had been closed.

A Japanese attack seemed so imminent at this time that even the larger hospital at Derby had been closed and temporarily moved thirty miles out of town to Meda Station. Very few white women remained in the Kimberley, Margaret and Mrs Bill MacDonald of Fossil Downs amongst them. Many others had long since moved away from the threatened far North.

Margaret's pregnancy had progressed normally. Nausea during those first months made her tasks in the kitchen more gruelling than ever. The relentless heat of October and November had seemed insufferable, but generally she had remained well and active, apart from the intermittent migraines that had plagued her all her life.

She continued to cope with her daily workload. The wet season arrived, Christmas came and went, and with it the news that George was to caretake GoGo whilst Ted Millard went away on leave.

This proved a convenient arrangement for the couple from Cherrabun, for Margaret, having visited Dr. Oldmeadow only twice during her pregnancy, had been advised to travel to Perth for her confinement. Her ante-natal care had, by necessity, been scant, but the visiting Dr. Oldmeadow assured her all was going well and it was only remoteness that made a Perth delivery a necessary precaution.

The couple moved to GoGo. The Cherrabun natives went on 'walkabout' and the Japanese continued to threaten Northern Australia. In mid-February Margaret was driven from GoGo to Fitzroy Crossing, to await a plane to take her to Derby and thence south to Perth, where she was to stay with George's mother, Martha, until the birth. However, having been deposited in Fitzroy, she soon found that no plane was expected for some time. Margaret was obliged to stay at the Post Office until its arrival.

She was feeling out of sorts and irritated by this turn of events. It seemed to her a most unsatisfactory arrangement, George across the Fitzroy river at GoGo, whilst she spent long idle days, cumbersome and hot, languishing at the Post Office. She was reliant on the hospitality of her hosts and chafing at her loss of independence. How much more enjoyable her sojourn might have been had Alice still been at the Hospital, but this was now closed and deserted, the few medical supplies and equipment having been commandeered by Bill MacDonald, head of the Local Defence Force.

Unlike the previous February when she had been married whilst the whole Fitzroy Crossing Valley was under flood, little rain fell during this February of 1943.

As each dry day came and went Margaret's restlessness grew, until finally she sent word to GoGo begging George to come and fetch her. 'The days are so dry' she pleaded, 'And GoGo is close to town. The river is low and easily passable. Why can't I wait for a plane over there with you?' George had to admit that it was unseasonably dry, and already missing Margaret's companionship, agreed to collect her for the remaining days before she was able to fly south.

♦ ♦ ♦

Margaret pulled the plaid blanket closer about her shoulders and rolled awkwardly onto her back. She could hear George still pacing back and forth on the verandah outside. The bulge of her belly obscured her view of him, but the intermittent mauve flashes of lightening that lit up the ceiling above her, showed his hauntingly large shadow against the far wall as he kept up his vigil during the night.

The sound of heavy raindrops hammering on the tin roof drowned all other noises of the night, except for the deep, rolling thunder crashing about the ridges not far away. The rain had started on the evening of her return to GoGo, three nights before, and had continued ever since. What seemed at first to be a seasonal late storm, had developed into a deep low over the West Kimberley. The relentless downpour had lasted through the night and all the following day.

By the second day Margaret knew her husband to be in one of his darkest moods. His brow as thunderous as the distant horizon, he snapped at the least aggravation, was curt during meals and restlessly paced about the homestead for hours at a time. Only once during the last three days had the rain eased off and then the racket of raindrops had been temporarily replaced by the chorus of frogs that always follow a torrential downpour. The lull had been short-lived however, and within an hour or two the heavens had opened again to drench the already sodden Fitzroy Valley.

Cherrabun

Lying awake that third wet night Margaret thought about the phone call George had received from Maxine MacDonald, on neighbouring Fossil Downs Station, just before they'd sat down to their evening meal. This had done nothing to improve his ill humour.

"What on earth can you be thinking of George, keeping your pregnant wife out there on the station?" Maxine had said.

"You must know the river is rising. It's already impassable, except by boat. You will have to get Margaret off GoGo soon George, or you will be delivering the baby yourself!"

Well aware of the awkwardness of the situation, and regretting each moment his acquiescence in allowing Margaret to leave the dull safety of the town Post Office, George was in no mood for criticism from his neighbour. He knew he must move Margaret into Fitzroy, but how was this to be achieved when the ground was saturated? There was no chance of getting a vehicle out to the road, let alone into town. He did not need telling. He already knew something must be done. He continued to pace back and forth, unaware that he was keeping his wife awake, while he pondered on their predicament.

At first light the weather appeared to have eased. Water lay everywhere, but few drops were breaking the sky reflecting surfaces. Frogs and cicadas were in full song. George looked tired and drawn, Margaret thought, as she gazed at him across the breakfast table. She felt sorry to have been the cause of so much worry. All she could do now was to agree readily to any plan he suggested.

"We'll have to ride over" He said, pushing back his chair as he rose from the table.

"It's about eight miles to the river. Do you think you can manage that?"

"I was brought up on a farm George, so I'm sure I will" she assured him, eager to make amends.

"Then we'll leave about noon. That will give it a few hours to clear up and time for you to get ready. I'll call up the Hotel and ask them to send the boat across to meet us. It will take a couple of hours you know. It'll be slow going for the horses. D'you really think you can do it?"

"I'll be fine George" she assured him

"Stop worrying"

He looked at her doubtfully.

"Riding about the farm as a kid isn't the same as slipping about on horseback seven months pregnant!"

"George, I will be fine. Don't worry" she retorted, trying not to sound impatient.

"Now let me tidy this meal up and I'll go and put my things together."

They left after an early lunch, about midday. Margaret mounted easily enough from the shed steps and settled herself into the stock saddle. It felt good to be on horseback again after so many years. She was glad she'd been so emphatic about her ability to cope with the ride. She was feeling quite confident as they turned their horses away from the homestead and set off in the direction of the river. She was going to be fine, just fine.

It was not long before Margaret found that she was far from fine. The stirrup leathers chaffed her legs badly and it wasn't long before she was obliged to tell George of her discomfort. He had rolled a spare pair of trousers, for his return journey, tied to the pommel of his saddle. He tossed these to Margaret and told her to put them on.

She dismounted and hauled them up under her dress. They were too long in the leg and she was unable to fasten them about her swollen middle. It was difficult for her to remount in her condition and clad in cumbersome clothing. George gave her a leg up, and was thankful to get her safely back in the saddle. He decided they would have to forego the afternoon tea they had brought with them. Although it would break the journey, he would not run the risk of allowing her to dismount again. He set his jaw firmly at Margaret's aggrieved look. He was not to be coerced a second time into pampering to her whims.

Cherrabun

It was a long tedious ride, full of discomfort and fraught with potential hazards. Now that the rain had stopped the air was alive with insects, mostly flies and mosquitoes, all causing acute annoyance. The water lay six to eight inches deep along the way, making it slow treacherous going and George, his experienced eye ever watchful for the firmer ground, was constantly fearful that his wife's horse might stumble or slip in the sodden conditions.

The humidity was extreme and both riders and mounts were damp from heat and perspiration. The sky was overcast and threatening. Margaret, looking at the inhospitable landscape about her, felt as though the clouds were pressing down upon them, almost close enough to touch, just waiting to dowse her in another deluge. She was supremely uncomfortable. Her large heavy body felt awkward on the hard saddle, her horse lacking the usual soothing rhythmic movement she'd associated with riding in the past. Sloshing and quivering to disperse the constantly nagging swarms of flies then sloshing on again. Fretfully tossing heads from side to side, the horses proceeded onwards toward the dark green timbered line of the valley that showed the snake like path of the mighty Fitzroy River. On and on they rode, mostly in silence, Margaret holding herself as erect as possible, to ease the stitch in her side, determined above all not to let George know of her discomfort.

At last they arrived at the riverbank. George dismounted first. Tethering his horse to a nearby tree, he stepped over to help Margaret dismount. Thankful at last to be out of the hard saddle, Margaret was surprised to find her legs barely able to support her. She was stiff and aching. Her legs felt weak and her buttocks sore. She left George to tie up her horse and wasted no time in discarding the heavy khaki trousers from under her dress. Feeling instantly cooler and more herself she looked about her. The river at this point was divided into two channels, the first part closest to them was still dry, but the second channel was flowing strongly, swift and deep.

"Are you right?" George asked his wife, taking the trousers from her, rolling them neatly as he spoke. "We'd better walk across and wait for the boat, it doesn't seem to be here yet."

Manoeuvring herself carefully down the slippery bank, Margaret trudged across the wide expanse of deep river sand which made up the bed of the dry channel. Even the short distance was tough going for her, as she heaved herself along. Effortlessly George strode beside her, one hand under her elbow, his dark rimmed eyes constantly glancing downstream to watch for the coming boat.

At last they were there. On the edge of the flowing channel and kneeling down in the river sand Margaret cupped her hands, bent her head and drank long and deeply of the muddy floodwater. Having quenched her thirst, she arranged herself comfortably in the shade of a paperbark tree and waited. George too, squatted in the shade. Together they listened idly to the rhythmic flow of the river, watching the frothing creamy bubbles eddying around a caught up branch, whose twigs in turn caught up other debris floating with the current downstream.

They waited, and they waited. The afternoon wore on, but still no boat came.

Presently a white haired native passed by on their side of the river. He was naked to the waist and carried a small sapling over his shoulder. His gait was purposeful but unhurried as he went by, with no sign or word of acknowledgement. Margaret wondered if his sight was poor, or perhaps, as was more usual, his shyness of white man prevented him from greeting them. They watched him walk out of sight before George spoke.

"Do you know who that was?" he asked.

"No, I don't" she replied

"Should I? He gave no sign of knowing us."

"You know him all right, Margaret" George said.

"That was Junkabine. He's going to get us the boat."

"How do you know that" Margaret asked, perplexed, as she tried to visualize the face from her nursing days. Junkabine, he was the man with pneumonia, who had insisted on wearing six shirts. Yes, that was Junkabine, but how white haired he had become since then.

"Get us the boat George?" she repeated absently.

"How can he do that?"

"Well you saw the sapling he was carrying? He'll use that to float himself downstream and when it strikes the far bank he'll get out and walk to the hotel to fetch the boat. That small tree will help him to keep afloat. He'll be back presently."

Margaret was sceptical, but refrained from voicing her doubts. How could Junkabine know they were waiting for the boat, without a word passing between them? Even if he had deduced as much, why would he bother to come to their aid if he did not have to?

Lost in thought she settled back against the paperbark's flaking trunk and closed her eyes. She felt weary. It had been a long gruelling afternoon and she had slept little the previous night. She vaguely wondered what they would do if the boat did not come to collect them, but she was too weary to worry much about anything at present. The sound of the water was soothing and in no time at all she drifted off into an untroubled sleep.

"He's coming Margaret" George nudged her gently.

"Wake up. Are you feeling better?" he asked looking down at her from where he stood. She stretched and taking his proffered hand, strong, brown and reassuring, allowed herself to be pulled to her feet.

Brushing the sand and leaves from the back of her crumpled frock she looked across the muddy water to where a small boat was being rowed towards them by the snowy haired native man.

Something in George's manner prevented her from voicing her surprise. His quiet sense of certainty had amused her, but now she felt humbled. How little she knew of these people. How in tune with them her husband was. This lesson she'd learned on the river bank would stay with her for many years to come. She who had been reared so far from here, educated, trained and dispatched to the remote West Kimberley was always so self assured and purposeful. She had felt advantaged, knowledgeable and more experienced than those about her. She had believed she and Alice knew more. They had come here to help, to show by example, to guide and encourage. Yet here she was suddenly made to realize how little she knew in reality, of what went on in the minds of these people of the outback. The silent language of the bush, the give and take of the one to the other, the pride and respect of each for their two different cultures. Yet George understood. Big, silent, implacable George, he had known, without so much as a sign.

There was much to be thought on resulting from this little episode. Margaret felt a good deal less self assured as she clambered aboard the small rowboat wobbling uncertainly beneath her weight. The sense of amazement stayed with her well after they had alighted safely at the foot of the hotel steps on the far side of the fast flowing river.

CHAPTER ELEVEN

First Baby

1943

Martha Poole, or Nana Wells as she was known by her family, was a tall upright woman, formidable in stance and stature, rigidly uncompromising and direct of speech. In short she was plainly forbidding, especially in the eyes of her young daughter-in-law, who was now staying with her.

Hardened, and slightly embittered, by her difficult years in the Kimberley, Martha had known tragedy. The death of two children and the loss of her brother, George Poole, had taken their toll and despite a move south to the comparative comfort of Perth she still found herself counting the cost of her years at Fitzroy Crossing.

She and her husband Billy had bought themselves a modest but durable little house in Nedlands some years earlier. This they shared together, when the latter was not away on his annual pilgrimages to the cattle camps of the North. After Billy's death in 1941 Martha's eldest son, George, took over the final payments due on the dwelling, where she now lived alone. Martha enjoyed her solitude, broken only by the occasional visits of her daughters Nora and Edna. Nora, her eldest girl had married Archibald Douglas, an orchardist and son of a West Australian Police commissioner. They lived on a pretty fruit farm in the hills region of Roleystone. Edna, the youngest surviving daughter, a staunch Catholic afflicted with a cleft palette, was married to a potato farmer from Vasse in the state's South West. Neither girl visited their mother often, but Nora, being closer, was the more frequent visitor of the two. Martha, left to her own devices, had learned to enjoy a measure of peace and solitude only dreamt of during the tough years of her early married life.

George Wells and his mother Martha, outside the Commonwealth bank building, Murray Street, Perth. 1941

Martha was somewhat irritated to find herself obliged to accommodate George's young wife, who, pregnant as she was, would undoubtedly disrupt the smooth running of the house. Why George had wanted to go and get married, at his time of life, she had no idea, but to have chosen a forthright young nurse, fifteen years his junior seemed to her the height of folly. Well, she supposed she would have to put up with it and there was only a short time until Margaret's expected confinement.

First Baby

The house in Clifton Street, situated well away from the fashionable riverside mansions for which Nedlands is best known, lay in a quiet back street close to the Hollywood Hospital. Built of brick with stuccoed walls and timbered verandahs, both front and back, it stood in a beautiful neat garden, small but carefully tended. It comprised two small bedrooms, lounge and kitchen, with a privy at the far end of the back yard, beyond the pomegranate and lemon trees.

Since summer had barely drawn to a close and March nights could still be warm and airless, Martha liked to sleep on the back verandah where there was a cool breeze. This arrangement, though sensible in itself, posed a problem for her guest that proved insoluble.

Advanced as she was into her pregnancy, Margaret was finding it increasingly difficult to pass the night without making several visits 'down the back' to the privy. Try as she would, she found it impossible to creep silently over the creaking timber boards. Nightly her heart sank as she passed through her mother-in-law's verandah room, trying to slip unnoticed down the yard path. Martha invariably stirred just as Margaret stepped silently down to the lawn, asking unnecessarily "Is that you again Margaret?" Thus successfully ensuring her visitor was aware that yet another disturbance had been registered by the old lady. But nothing prepared her for the evening that the pains started. First barely more than gentle tightenings, they had increased until Margaret timidly broached the subject with Martha.

"Well?" her mother-in-law exclaimed

"You had better get yourself to the hospital right away. I don't want you having the baby here, so hurry along."

There was no telephone in the house so Margaret set off to walk down the street to the corner phone box. It was quite dark as she stepped outside, despite wartime daylight saving, and the black-out conditions occasioned meant that no lights were visible to illuminate her way. It was a short distance and in a few minutes she was letting herself through the heavily swung door of the telephone kiosk. She had timed her walk to leave the house at the conclusion of a contraction and hoped to make her call to the hospital, requesting they send a taxi, before the next pain commenced. It was with some dismay, that she found the phone to be out of order, and pausing to lean against the heavy glass wall she contemplated her next move.

Boley's Bakery, where she frequently bought bread for her mother-in-law, lay on the opposite side of the road, and despite the darkness Margaret knew the family would be hard at work inside preparing dough for the next day. She crossed over to the corner shop, going silently through the back gate so as not to disturb the dogs and thus the neighbourhood.

"I'm sorry to trouble you" she began as several startled faces looked up at her approach.

"The telephone is out of order over the road and I need to ring the hospital. I wonder if you'd be kind enough to let me use yours." She said, proffering some coins as she spoke.

"Well, yes, - I s'pose so" the proprietor agreed.

"It's out in the passageway. Here show the lady where to go" he added giving a nearby youngster a floury push toward the door.

Margaret lifted the receiver as the boy left, and prepared to call King Edward Memorial Hospital, but at this moment she felt the onset of another contraction and quickly replaced the receiver. Breathing slowly and deeply she waited for the pain to pass before finally making her call.

During the war years it was difficult to get a cab. Due to petrol rationing city taxis were only used for essential journeys, buses and trams being the main form of public transport. Margaret was therefore obliged to explain her position to the hospital who then were able to authorize a vehicle to come and collect her. At the conclusion of her call she left a few coins beside the phone and called a 'thank you' as she let herself out quietly and hurried back up the street toward No. 29. It was two hours short of midnight. The day, April 9th, 1943.

First Baby

The static over the radio made it difficult to hear. George caught only the last of the message.

'Gram from Perth, are you reading? Over'

'Yes reading O.K. Go ahead, Over' George responded, straining to catch what he guessed would be a communication from either Emanuel Brothers or Margaret.

'Boy arrived safely, wearing black .....' A broad smile lit up his face. George barely heard the remainder of the telegram. So it was a son and not a redhead after all. Good. Absent mindedly he terminated his sched. and walked outside into the steamy sunlight. Well done Margaret, he thought. George was quietly pleased with the message his wife had sent. She had feared that her baby might be a redhead, especially after he had told her that his father had red hair in his youth.

"I don't want our children to have his colouring in this climate" she had said aggrieved.

As nothing was private over the radio he understood why she worded her telegram as she had. Little did he know that his neighbour, Maxine Macdonald, had misinterpreted the cable and was agitatedly thinking that Margaret's baby had been stillborn. Furthermore she was wondering whether this had been caused by the desperate ride to the river a few weeks earlier. Surely 'wearing black' could only mean one thing,

Meanwhile, in Perth Margaret was congratulating herself on her forethought and good sense, for despite the rather tardy appearance of her mother-in-law she had still managed to get messages sent from her hospital bed with the good news. Always prepared for any eventuality she had taken with her, carefully packed in her small bag, several blank telegram forms. These she had sent out with one of the more amiable staff at the hospital, to her mother and sister in New South Wales, George at Fitzroy Crossing and Alice Hall in Sydney.

"And is this a 'Little Blossom In The Dust', or a "Rosebud"? asked the carefully starched sister now standing at the end of the bed looking at her notes.

"You don't get many visitors do you dear?"

'Blossom In The Dust' thought Margaret indignantly. She was a respectably married woman, not a mother left in the lurch by a visiting American serviceman.

"A Rosebud" she responded shortly. "My husband is man-powered up North" and she turned onto her side, pointedly presenting her back to the talkative, over inquisitive nurse.

Margaret's journey home was difficult to say the least and took, in all, upwards of a week.

Having spent several trying weeks at Clifton Street with Nanna Wells, she booked a seat with MacRobertson Miller Airlines on a bi-plane piloted by Captain Cyril Kleinig. She had caught the MMA bus from their city terminal out to the airport, and along with seven or eight other passengers clambered aboard the aircraft. It was still early and the May morning was chilly. Margaret tightened the shawl about her infant and easing herself into the small aircraft found a seat. Having stowed the luggage and seen his passengers on board, Captain Kleinig approached Margaret carrying a canvas bag.

"Here, put your feet on this Mrs Wells. You'll be more comfortable" He told her, wedging the cumbersome carry-all beneath her seat. She rested her feet on it.

"It's the tool kit" he said, "But it'll be all right as a foot rest."

Soon afterwards they were airborne, the small plane dipping and rising on the air currents as they lifted over the Darling escarpment and headed North on the first leg of their long journey. It was bitterly cold in the plane, but baby John lay peacefully in his mother's arms, oblivious to her discomfort. Margaret thankful to find him so easily settled cuddled him closely to her chest and tried to forget about her frozen feet and the cramped conditions that made movement an impossibility.

They flew for most of the day, reaching the small coastal town of Onslow late in the afternoon. Here the passengers alighted and were transported to the local hotel for the night. Margaret had bought a folding pram before leaving Perth which she carried upstairs to her room. She felt exhausted and her arms were stiff from the constant cradling of her baby, so it was a relief for her to settle him in the pram. John, however was not happy. He was tired, damp and uncomfortable. He registered his displeasure by crying loudly and persistantly. Darkness had already fallen. Having travelled north beyond the tropic of Capricorn the lengthy twilights of Perth were behind them. Here the days ended abruptly with the setting sun and nightfall followed swiftly.

Margaret, as always prepared for any circumstance, felt for the small flashlight torch she carried with her and shining it down onto the furious infant prepared to change the offending nappy. No sooner had she undone the first pin than the proprietoress marched boldly into the room with barely a courtesy knock.

"What do you think you are doing?" she enquired rudely as Margaret looked up in surprise.

"Signalling to ships from the window I suppose" she accused, as she strode across and snatched the blackout curtains together. Margaret, erect now, her indignation rising, was speechless with amazement.

"Don't you know there's a war on?" the irate woman continued

"Haven't you heard of black-out" and she marched out of the room slamming the door behind her.

Angry as she was Margaret soon realized nothing was to be gained by falling out with the disagreeable woman. What she needed was a meal and a good night's rest. She finished changing the baby and settled herself comfortably against the bed-head to feed him. Her eyelids drooped with fatigue as she absently fondled the tiny pink foot protruding from the blue knitted shawl. How good it would be to get home at last, she thought. How proud George would be of her and this beautiful boy. The Lord had been good to them, as she had known he would be, and she lapsed into an informal silent prayer of thanks for this her most recent blessing.

Their journey continued all the next day, as far as Broome. Here they were delayed for a week. There were very few women in Broome at this time, the tiny pearling town having been harassed by the Japanese and under continuing threat. Only Mrs Knight, matron of the native hospital, Blue Lloyd and the manager's wife of the Governor Hotel, with whom Margaret stayed, were still resident in the town.

Major Mitchell, who was Commander of the Armed Forces in the North at this time, was joined by his wife and young baby who had flown up on the same plane with Margaret. Mrs Mitchell was in some distress upon their arrival at Broome, with the discovery that her thirteen cocktail hats had been mislaid on the journey. Her concern was incomprehensible to Margaret, who had never conformed to fashionable trends of any kind. Margaret's worries lay in another direction and when she was invited to accompany a small party on a sight seeing tour of the town she refused explaining that she had a baby to look after. Mrs Mitchell suggested that Margaret could also look after her baby for her, so that she could join the tour. Margaret agreed.

A few days later Margaret was flown from Broome to Fitzroy Crossing where Ted Millard and George met her. Much to Margaret's delight Grace and Bill Henwood had sent a meat-safe cot from Noonkenbah on one of the military vehicles. She had never considered the need for a mosquito proof cot for baby John, having so far made do with the pram. It was a sturdy piece of furniture, encased with fly wire and was an invaluable addition to their possessions.

After greeting Margaret warmly, the two men took her and the other passengers up to the hotel for a meal of steak. Seated at the table, trying to cut up the Kimberley beef with a baby in her arms proved more than Margaret could manage, so having waited for George to finish his meal, she passed John across to him.

"Here George, you hold the baby now, so I can eat my meal" she said.

George looked acutely embarassed and uncomfortable. He grappled with his small son and endeavoured to secure him in his grasp.

"What do you think of him?" Margaret asked, as George continued to struggle with the squirming infant.

"Well, not much Margaret." he whispered to her quietly.

"It's a much better baby over there" and he indicated with a sideways nod the further end of the room. Margaret looked over to the only other child she could see. 'What's wrong with the man?' she thought, as her eyes alighted unbelievingly on a ten month old child lying motionless on the table where its mother sat eating. Margaret chewed her steak slowly, wondering if her husband was serious or not.

"Why don't you just put John down on the table top like that?" he asked her.

"Because he wouldn't stay there for five minutes" she snapped.

"That other baby is spastic George. It's severely handicapped, ten months old and cannot move" George looked at her shocked

"It's true George. John is only two months old and he might be wriggling and squirming like a little worm, but he's healthy, and he's normal. Give him to me, I've eaten as much as I want."

So this was the welcome she had so longed for. Perhaps they would all settle more comfortably together once they reached the station she thought and turning once more to George she said with a good deal more kindness

"When can we leave for Cherrabun George? I just want to get home."

They set off during the afternoon, having first collected the mail and a few essential supplies needed on the station. When they were within a mile of the homestead the vehicle spluttered ominously and ground to a halt. George announced, matter of factly, that they had run out of gas.

Hughie Bent, or the 'mad mechanic' as he was usually called, made gas by some process, not fully understood by Margaret, involving the burning of wood. This had helped tide the Emanuel stations over the war years of petrol rationing, but on occasion the gas supply was not sufficient to complete the longer journeys undertaken. Fortunately George and Margaret were so near home they were able to unload the pram and to wheel baby John over the last bumpy mile.

Margaret had grown to like Cherrabun. The river close to the homestead and the hills, so unlike those of New England, were a joy to her. She did not like the vast flat expanses that stretched between Fitzroy Crossing and Derby and had been mightily relieved on that first occasion when George had shown her her new home in those earliest days of their engagement.

It was June, the coolest time of the year in the North West. The days were mild, the evenings quite chilly and strong Easterly winds blew from the desert to set the river gums tossing and swaying against the clear cerulean sky.

Margaret was happy. She quickly settled into the usual busy routine of station life. George was frequently away for days on end, it being the height of the mustering season and so it was Margaret who first heard over the peddle set radio that Gordon Smith, the Emanuel's manager at Meda, had been killed whilst mustering. Details had been sketchy, but it appeared he had been thrown from his horse and had struck an antbed when he fell. They were both understandably shaken by this accident and Margaret, tired by the day, was preparing to go to bed.

George glanced up at his wife as she made her way toward the door.

"Margaret" he halted her "There's something I have to tell you" and seeing her surprised look he continued with a note of firmness

"Emanuels are sending me to Meda to replace Gordon Smith."

Margaret, looking at her husband, saw the firm set of his jaw that she recognised meant he'd brook no argument. She knew there was no choice to be made. If Emanuel Brothers needed George at Meda there they would go. Neither his feelings, nor her wishes, mattered. No use saying how much she preferred Cherrabun, she thought. Meda was flat, that was all she knew about it, and it had a fine homestead, said to be the pride of Isadore Emanuel.

'I shall have to make the best of it she thought to herself. 'Dear God, help us on this next leg of life, and keep George from harm'.

"When do we go?" she asked heavily, suddenly feeling more weary than usual.

"Now " George responded bluntly. "I know you've only been back a month Margaret, but they need someone there right away."

"And who will come here in our place?" she asked

"Well, I understand Harry Scrivener will take over" George told her. "He'll be o.k."

Ted Millard, as seemed so often to be the case, came once more to George and Margaret's aid. They had, soon after their marriage, purchased a few pieces of furniture from the Post Master at Fitzroy Crossing, namely a double bed, lowboy, kitchen table and two chairs. Furniture was not provided by Emanuels at this time. The difficulty of removing their modest collection of possessions the two hundred miles or so across to Meda had seemed insurmountable to the young mother who was so reluctantly packing up at Cherrabun. When Ted Millard offered them the use of Emanuels' only truck Margaret was again grateful for his kindness to them. Ever since she had first arrived in the Kimberley it seemed Mr Millard had been there to help. They would miss him a great deal now they were to live so far from GoGo.

The day came, all too soon for Margaret, when the last bag was closed and loaded onto the truck. With George at the wheel, herself and the infant beside him, they rumbled their way slowly up the dusty access track away from Cherrabun for the last time.

Standing outside the homestead, waving, stood George's replacement, Harry Scrivener, and his wife Nan. Harry was a tall, gentle man. He had been working for Emanuels on Meda Station from the age of sixteen. Now in his late twenties he had courted and married young Nan from Ellendale and they had one child. Nan was a slightly built girl, bright, cheerful and garrulous to the point of irritation. They would fair well together, Margaret thought, casting a brief glance behind her. The cloud of dust thrown up by the truck tyres all but obliterated her view of the diminishing figures at the gate, but she nonetheless waved with her free hand and did her best to cast her thoughts ahead rather than behind.

"Wake him George and get him to move!" Margaret spoke reprovingly, unable to suppress her irritation a moment longer.

"He's blocking the road, and if he's drunk it's his fault, not ours" she added.

George showed no sign whatever of hearing her. He was not going to argue with her, especially in front of the other passengers. He simply pretended he was deaf. He clambered down from the truck.

"Pass us the axe Jack" he spoke up to the young half caste lad on the back. Jack Shaw was a youth of about nineteen whom they had picked up at GoGo, where they had spent the previous night. He was a bright, useful boy whom Ted Millard had entrusted with the job of returning the truck after transporting the Wells' to Meda. Jack rummaged briefly through the packing cases before finding the axe and a shovel. Passing the former to George, he jumped down lightly.

"What are you going to do George?" Margaret asked, standing close by the bonnet looking in amazement at her husband.

First Baby

"We'll cut some saplings and make another crossing" George told her shortly.

"Jack Green might be drunk, but I'm not waking him Margaret. We'll let him sleep it off in peace and go round him instead."

'And that's that', thought Margaret, no matter the unnecessary delay. Little did she realize how much more trouble Jack Green would be, if woken, than making another crossing would prove.

They had made their way from GoGo through the back of Brooking Springs towards Ellendale. There had been a fall of winter rain in the area and some parts of the dirt track required caution to avoid bogging. It was at one such wet area that they had met with the present obstacle. The small creek would have been easily traversable had it not been for Jack Green sleeping off his intoxication across the front seat of his vehicle.

Apart from Jack Shaw, who was now assisting George in creating a firm enough bed of bush and saplings over which to drive the truck, the young couple had brought along two passengers from Cherrabun. Hansen Boxer, a toddler of about two years, and his mother, a small boned full blood native, nick-named Spino Shanks on account of her spindly limbs, were also travelling with them. Hansen had met with an accident recently, burning all the skin off his fingers, which were now carefully bound in vaseline gauze.

The injury needed careful attention to avoid infection and so Margaret had decided to take the child and his mother down to the native hospital at Derby. Hansen's father, Boxer, a tall, fine looking pindan native, had been most reluctant to allow his wife and child to go. Jack Shaw was 'geegul' to Spino Shanks and much persuasion had been needed before Boxer finally consented to Margaret's persistent coaxing. They were a wretched looking pair, perched on top of the loaded truck. Hansen, his poor burnt hand held gingerly away from him to avoid any unnecessary pain, his mother seated beneath him, her eyes downcast, silent, sullen and fearful.

It was not long before George declared the rough and ready crossing substantial enough to bear the truck safely and the party continued on its way. The heavily laden conveyance with its unlikely assortment of passengers made slow progress along the narrow bumpy track. Soon they decided to call it a day and George pulled up for the night.

Camping on the ground, John comfortable in his pram, they spent the night sleeping under the stars, as all but Margaret had done for most of their lives. She alone lay restlessly listening to the night noises of the bush. A lone beast bellowing in the distance, the eerie call of a stone curlew and the constant gusting wind that set the canvas flapping, all contributed to her wakefulness.

In the grey light of dawn, when George rose to stir the campfire she too rose, stiff, sandy and sadly disheveled, to face another day on the road. She fed and changed John, rinsing his napkins in a pan of water and holding them out of the truck window to dry as they rumbled laboriously towards Ellendale.

Here they pulled up for lunch, a delicious meal of spinach and meatballs, prepared by the Bell's half caste help Dora Watson. As they prepared to leave Ellendale, Mrs Bell came to Margaret carrying a small tin of cocoa which she tucked under the young mother's arm.

"Here Margaret, take this" she said

"You may well be glad of it later." Grateful indeed for such kindness Margaret thanked her. She felt considerably refreshed since she'd eaten. Climbing once more into the high passenger seat she was able to view the forthcoming drive with a good deal more optimism. She had been enchanted by Mrs Bell's Pekinese dogs, who had danced to the cylinder gramophone. All in all she had enjoyed their brief visit and had much to think about as they drove on, in silence, towards Blina.

At Blina she was further surprised to find that an afternoon tea of saucer cakes had been prepared for them.

"Anyone would think you were expecting company" Margaret smilingly told Mr. Bowden as he passed her the plate.

First Baby

"Well Margaret, the bush telegraph keeps me informed," Don Bowden told her.

"I was told to expect company today"

Don Bowden was not a tall man, but darkly good looking, well spoken and intelligent. He was the son of an accountant and had done accountancy himself, though finding it a tedious occupation had sought employment elsewhere and come to the bush. He was in his late twenties and still a bachelor. It was a sad business how few suitable women there were for these able bodied men of the North, Margaret thought, not for the first time. Perhaps less of them would turn to drink had they a wife and the comforts of a good home to keep them contented. Little was she to know that Don Bowden was later to become her brother-in-law and a cherished member of the family.

Blina, a sheep station, was predominantly flat, with no large river system. It was exactly the type of country Margaret liked least. Glancing out across the endless flat land to the far distant horizon she found herself hoping Meda would not be like this.

No sooner were they back in the privacy of the truck than Margaret found herself voicing her fears to her husband.

"Has Meda got any hills George" she asked

"I liked the hills at Cherrabun and this place looks so dreary"

"Oh yes, it's got a couple" George assured her. He did not add that neither were large enough to notice, unless you rode up alongside them. 'One Tree' was no more than a rocky outcrop rising from miles of surrounding plain, and 'Yarrada', though slightly more significant, was located close to the river and in such a position as to go easily unnoticed.

"And rivers?" Margaret questioned.

"Well yes, there are rivers. Of course there are rivers. The May and the Meda and lots of channel country. You'll like it Margaret." He assured her, adding as an afterthought "and you'll be closer to town than we were on Cherrabun."

They were grinding slowly down over a ridge where the track, having deteriorated somewhat, required George's closer attention and conversation ceased between them for a time.

"Blina's boundary runs onto Meda" George commented as he shifted up a gear at the foot of the ridge,

"We should be there by nightfall"

"Look, a hill! George. Is that on Meda?" Margaret pointed ahead eagerly.

"No that's Mount Marmion on Kimberley Downs" he told her.

"K.D's only a small place, but good country I'm told. That's where Jack Lee is. It's owned by M.C. Davies as well"

"As well as what" Margaret questioned.

"Blina. They own both places, and Napier Downs" Again they lapsed into silence.

The sun by this time was low on the horizon, the sky a subtle blend of rose and violet. Wispy fingers of smoke tainted the evening sky forming thought provoking images beyond the intricate tracery of bare branches silhouetted against the glorious backdrop.

"Looks like that bushfire's on Meda" George commented, breaking into Margaret's thoughts.

"I hope they've got onto it. These easterlies won't be helping." he added, a note of concern clearly detectable in his voice.

There seemed little to add to these observations, though Margaret's pleasurable contemplation of the evening sky was considerably diminished by his remarks. She sat in silence cradling John, who lay sleeping comfortably on her lap, and patiently endured the final hour of their long journey.

CHAPTER TWELVE

Meda
1943

They had arrived dusty, weary and apprehensive at the end of that memorable day, to find that the bushfire they had watched anxiously during their final approach to Meda was licking about the fence posts having earlier threatened the homestead itself.

They were greeted by Andy Anderson, Emanuel's man from Perth, who had been despatched to Meda by head office as soon as news of Gordon Smith's death was received. He had been taking care of the most pressing affairs of the station during the intervening weeks since the tragedy and was delighted by the arrival of the new manager, who could now be expected to take over the reins. The fire, which had been an additional burden, was more or less under control, the inhabitants having back burnt off the tracks and cattle pads so the immediate danger was passed.

After the initial introductions had been made George and Margaret were shown into the station kitchen where Mrs. Smith, the grief stricken widow, was valiantly attending to her final duties on Meda. Here an evening meal was ready for the travellers. Under a protective net cover stood a platter of cold beef, potatoes and a glass of crisp white shallots. A kerosene lamp was in the centre of the table on an upturned cake tin and two lanterns stood on either side of the stove where Mrs Smith was pouring boiling water into a large, chipped enamel teapot.

After the meal Mrs Smith took Margaret over to the house, showing her along a wide timber verandah to a sleep-out and bedroom at the far side of the building. Parking John's pram at the end of the unmade bed, Margaret asked where she could find some bed linen.

"I'm afraid it's all locked up" the widow told her.

"Mr Anderson has been seeing to all that sort of thing. I'm sorry, I didn't give it a thought, but it's all been so ...." and her voice trailed away into a poorly concealed sob, as she turned and hurried from the room.

Margaret looked about her. Beyond the flywire walls of the sleepout grew a thick tangle of flowering creeper. She could smell the heady scent of quis-qualis and green, twirling tendrils of Mexican rose could be seen twining about the thick woody stems. Margaret bent over the pram and lifted John up. She had brought one spare double sheet with her to place in the baby's pram, and this she now retrieved and spread across the bed. She settled John for the night and there still being no sign of George, whom she had last seen in deep conversation with Mr. Anderson, went to bed herself. She did not hear her husband come in. The exhaustion which had been with her all that long day at last dissipated. She fell soundly asleep.

The following morning, long before the sun had risen above the low smoke clouded horizon, the inhabitants were again assembled in the station kitchen to eat the usual pre-dawn breakfast that preceded each busy day. It was to be a day of intense activity at the homestead, which saw the unloading and placing of the Wells' modest possessions from the back of the truck. The table and chairs had been deposited by Margaret in a small corner sleep-out that she intended to use as a dining room for herself and George. She did not like eating meals with the men, preferring to use meal times for some much needed private conversation with her husband. She oversaw the delivery of the wardrobe and lowboy into one of the inside bedrooms, likewise their double bed. She then set about unpacking some clothes, needed for immediate use, before going to ask George how Spino Shanks and Hansen could best be delivered to the native hospital in town.

Meda

During the morning Mrs. Gordon Smith, who had been tearfully stowing her few more personal possessions into her car, prepared to leave Meda. Margaret waved her off with some relief. Although she pitied her deeply her early departure seemed to be the most sensible course of action.

The third departure for the day was that of Jack Shaw in the GoGo truck, and with the dust on the road settling behind him, Margaret, at last, felt ready to aquaint herself with her new surroundings. She met Ngungala and Dora, the two stout native girls who were assigned to assist in the kitchen. George had been closeted for much of the morning with Mr Anderson, perusing the station horse book, stock records and bore book.

The homestead, essentially a large square structure, timber built with an iron roof, was elevated two or three feet above ground level by means of sturdy timber struts. Wide wooden verandahs, enclosed at the four corners with flywire screens to form sleep-outs, were largely concealed by a lattice of dense creeper which added to the cool shady appearance of the dwelling. At the centre of the homestead lay three small rooms, evidently used as bedrooms during the cooler months. A slightly larger room, with decorative plastered ceiling formed a serviceable, though hardly elegant, sitting room. Concrete steps led down from the verandahs on all sides, one of which gave onto a short pathway leading to an outside ablution block. This, Margaret discovered, still had an old fashioned bucket toilet, but otherwise the homestead was impressive and much as she had been led to believe.

It was built on rising ground of coffee rock, overlooking a large tree lined billabong where numerous waterbirds could be seen feeding and wading at the muddy edge. Beyond the billabong lay an expanse of parched bare ground, or 'scalded flat', as George called it, where the occasional swollen trunked boab tree blossomed with flocks of noisy white corellas.

On the top side of the homestead the ground rose away toward an horizon of burnt scrub. Broken outcrops of pindan coloured coffee rock showed rusty red amongst the black and white traces of yesterday's fire, where fallen timbers lay still smoking in jagged disarray over the rough bare ground.

The brightest patch of colour in this desolate scene was the green expanse of a thriving vegetable patch. Here Margaret was cheered to find pumpkin vines, neat rows of onions, lettuce and beetroot together with tomato plants just coming into flower and the remains of what had clearly been a good crop of cabbages, all growing strong and healthy in the coolest, driest month of the year. Bamboos grew in profusion close by the station water tanks, the easterly breeze making them rustle and sway as she passed.

The station kitchen was separate, though not far distant, from the house and to the east of this were the men's quarters. The native camp was further over still, with the goat yard beyond. To the right of the goat yard was a timber stockyard, horse stable and saddle room. Various sheds, workshop and a blacksmith's shed lay back towards the kitchen where a spinifex and wire netting meathouse completed the small group of buildings that made up the Meda homestead.

The native camp was considerably smaller than that at Cherrabun, with only about two dozen natives living there. Mustering had temporarily come to a halt since the death of the manager and so the full compliment of Meda's native population was in at the station when Margaret and George arrived.

The day was now well advanced. Margaret headed back toward the house. John would need to be changed and fed before she served the next meal and there were napkins to be rinsed and others to bring in from the line. Having done this she returned to the kitchen to prepare tea. Mrs Smith had seen to the bread making early that morning, but tomorrow Margaret must take up her role in earnest and it was clear that her days would be long and full.

The day began on Meda at half past three in the morning, with Margaret one of the earliest to stir. The daily task of bread making was the first chore, when a big fire would be made in the mud brick oven outside the kitchen. Bread was made for everyone on the station, not only those that ate in the station kitchen but for the native camp as well. When the brick oven was good and hot, Margaret, or one of the native girls, would remove the coals so that the dough, proven and risen in black, well used tins, could be put in to cook. In later years a big wood stove with two ovens was installed in the station kitchen. This would be filled daily with bread to feed the station. Only when the stockcamp was out and there were less mouths to feed at home did Margaret occasionally have a day free of this task.

Breakfast was served at five o'clock each morning, this after a frantic race against time. The kitchen was a buzz with activity, fires were lit, meals prepared, kettles boiled, bread made, tables set and floors swept. Finally a sound clang on the triangle hanging up outside forecast to all that the meal was served and ready.

In addition to the early morning ritual that took place in the kitchen, down at the goat's yard, each day unfolded with the task of morning milking. Margaret tried to ensure udders were washed prior to milking, and soon learnt to keep a keen eye open for basins of watered down milk. She discovered the natives' trick was to take half a basin of water with them to milk into. The milk was later shared amongst everyone. Try as she would, Margaret was never able to halt this practise. No end of chastisement seemed to deter the culprits from attempting the same thing a day or so later. Meda had a large number of goats. Used mainly for milk, they were also an important source of meat during the 'wet season' when monsoonal rains made it impossible to get a 'killer'.

In later years the station was supplied with a separator and having separated the cream and milk, they were able to make butter to supplement the tinned butter previously used. The goats butter was pure white and Margaret would add colouring to give it a more appealing appearance.

Despite this she was never able to convert George to the goats' butter, he complained of the smell of it and preferred to take his bread with jam or tinned butter. He would never have both, believing this to be unnecessarily extravagant. He was sparing in all things other than work. Luxury and self indulgence were unknown to him, with the exception of an occasional 'spree' when meeting with friends in town.

The work load on Meda was such that all those physically able were expected to share with the daily tasks. The goats, in addition to being milked, had to be minded when out of their yard during the day. This job was done by two or three of the older natives who also yarded them at night. Then there was the vegetable garden to be tended and watered. This arduous task was undertaken morning and evening so as not to run the risk of burning foliage in the heat of the day. Water was carried in buckets by means of a yoke worn about the shoulders and round the back of the neck. It was a system greatly disapproved of by Margaret. She was quick to confront George with her concerns and it was not long before a system of hoses was introduced that made lighter work for those natives given the task.

In addition to Ngungala and Dora, who helped Margaret in the kitchen, she was also assisted by Linda, the mother of two children and wife of Nugget. Her girls, Roslyn and Daisy, shy and giggly as any approaching puberty, with the dusky good looks and slender limbs of their race were also expected to do a share of raking and sweeping about the paths and buildings. Nugget had a second, younger wife called Maudie who was a girl of about sixteen. There were also two literate youths from Sunday Island, called Con and Willie, who were a similar age to Maudie. They worked with the men under George's supervision, as did Spider, reputedly a superb stockman who was married to Eileen. Eileen, or Eilie as she was more usually known was an immensely tall statuesque woman, so long limbed and with such outstandingly long fingers and toes as to be quite arresting. Other natives in the camp when Margaret and George first came to Meda included Nosey Paddy, Frank, an old girl called Topsy, Jimmy who had lost one eye as a boy in a spearing accident in long grass, Lulu and Old Nugget who was now well past his prime. There were, amongst these, natives in the camp, who for one reason or another were not called upon to work. These included

Blind Jack, Ngungala's father, and July who had a baby too young and troublesome to enable her to assist in any way. All were cared for, fed and clothed by the station, issued with weekly rations, daily bread and milk and any of their health needs attended to. It did not take long for Margaret to get to know them, and exasperating as she frequently found them, especially the pranks of Roslyn and Daisy, a fondness for each soon developed between them. A fondness that was to last a lifetime and in circumstances different from those of their first acquaintance.

An ominous grey haze on the horizon slowly rose above the tops of the intervening trees to leach the colour from the clear blue morning sky. The bushfire had started in the direction of the Leprosarium, somewhere beyond Number One Bore. From her vantage point on the homestead verandah, where she sat feeding John, it brought back memories to Margaret of her first evening at Meda.

The stockcamp, George with it, had been out for ten days taking the mustering cart laden with stores and the camp cook with them. Their departure, although lightening the workload at the homestead, had left Margaret feeling ill at ease. They had been on Meda only a few weeks and she was still coming to terms with her new position.

The homestead was situated on the road from Derby to Mount House and callers were frequent. She seemed to be constantly finding additional meals for unexpected visitors, some welcome, others less so. The stock route, that also ran close by Meda, brought extra pressures and Margaret was still unused to dealing with the demands of all those who passed by.

She was now confronted with a new problem. Clearly there was a bushfire towards the bullock paddock and no-one but the natives at home to advise her. Getting up from her chair she placed John in his customary position over her shoulder, and, patting him gently on the back, walked down the steps to get a better view of the smoke haze. She then saw a small delegation approaching from the direction of the native camp. She walked across to meet them, wondering as she did so what their trouble was now. Which picaninnie was ill or who wanted more sugar or bread before ration time. These were the usual demands to be coped with and so she was surprised to hear Old Nugget say,

"We gotta go pight 'im dat push pire Missus! Put 'im out" as he cast an unhurried glance in the direction of the smoke cloud, lifting his arm loosely from his side to point away beyond the billabong.

"You gonna bin dribe us Missus?" he added somewhat hopefully.

"Drive you!" exclaimed Margaret in surprise.

"I can't drive you down there in the car. What if I get it bogged?" Visions of getting stuck in one of the sandy creeks, breaking down, or worse still becoming lost, flashed before her. What about baby John? He was only a few months old. She could not risk being caught in the smoke with her baby. George had done nearly all the driving since she had known him. She had no idea how to negotiate the rough sandy tracks that were considered to be roads here in the North. She looked at the dark enquiring faces before her.

"I'm no good at driving that car Nugget." she told him, wondering when George might be back. She didn't really know where the stockcamp was, or when to expect them home again.

"Where's Brandy's?" she asked, this being the name of the area George had mentioned they were to muster before he had left.

"Ooh - long way Missus" the elderly native boy told her

"Ober dat riber, an' long way. We go down to dat pire an pix 'im Missus" he added

"How will you get there?" she asked

" We walk. Ngungala, she come too. Ngungala ride 'im dat mule eh?" Margaret uncertain whether this was a question or statement nodded her agreement. Yes, Ngungala was too big to walk any distance, it would be better if she could ride.

Relieved to be presented with this solution Margaret set about gathering a supply of bread and meat to send out with the band of fire fighters. There seemed to be quite an air of excitement amongst them, with all who were young enough and able, eager to go. Margaret was in some doubt about Ngungala's going with them. She was a large girl of about eighteen stone, but she seemed quite determined to join in the expedition so there was little Margaret could do without causing some upset amongst them.

It took a little while for the party to get ready. Billy cans, tea, sugar and tin pannikins were collected. Bread and meat was placed in flour bags. Eventually they set off, talking excitedly together, for all the world as if this were some wonderful picnic on which they were about to embark. Margaret watched them until they passed out of sight beyond the billabong, the bulk of them walking with the slow aimless gait she knew so well, Ngungala, like a queen, riding the mule alongside.

◆ ◆ ◆

George, having seen the smoke get up on the western horizon some two days earlier and with the mustering round completed at Brandy's, left instructions with his headstockman and made for home with all speed. It was a six hour ride cross-country for the new manager, the afternoon was well advanced by the time he came in sight of the homestead.

As he rode down the track that led to the station yard he was perplexed to find the native camp all but deserted. Only blind Jack was seated in the shade, a pair of dogs curled up asleep beside him. Stiff from long hours in the saddle, George dismounted, draping the reins over his arm, he loosened the girth and led his horse over to the water trough. Here he removed the heavy stock saddle, gave the mare a quick rub and unstrapping his quartpot used this to wash her down after her exertion. Then taking the bridle off he set her loose to feed. As he walked across from the men's quarters towards the kitchen he was further surprised to notice the limp leaves on the pumpkin vines which clearly had not been watered that morning.

Neither Dora nor Ngungala were in the kitchen, but the kettle was on the hob and some vegetables in a bowl were placed in readiness under a gauze cloth on the table. George left the building and headed up the footpath to the house. He was coated in fine dust, his clothes soiled with perspiration and dark stubble showed on his chin. He took the concrete steps in one stride, mounting the front verandah in some haste as his concern grew.

Margaret, who had just retrieved the day's washing from the line, looked up in surprise at the sound of riding boots crossing the timber boards.

"Why, hello George, I didn't know you were home!" she greeted him

"Is the stockcamp in as well? I wasn't expecting you yet"

"Where is everyone?" George interrupted

"The place is deserted. Where's Dora and Linda? and how come the vegetable garden is so dry?"

Margaret, hesitating in some confusion wondered how George could have taken in the state of affairs so quickly.

"What has brought you home in such a rush?" she asked, quite forgetting his series of enquiries.

"Well I saw that smoke get up over there, so I've come home to see about it" he told her.

"Where is everybody?" he asked again.

"Well they're out fighting the fire" she answered, feeling quite pleased with herself.

"So where's Ngungala" George questioned her.

"She's fighting the bush fire too." Margaret told him patiently. George stared at his wife in astonishment before commenting with a wry grin,

"What use would she be fighting bush fires Margaret? She's about eighteen stone. How did she get down there?"

"Well, she rode on the mule George."

"You NEVER put that weight on the mule!" George exploded, all humour vanishing.

"How did the rest go?"

"They walked" she told him.

"And the others said it would be all right for Ngungala to go on the mule" she tried to placate her irate husband.

He looked at her sternly, whilst Margaret waited for further comment. He was plainly furious, but thinking better of admonishing her he turned on his heel and strode off to the kitchen. Margaret deposited her armful of clean washing on the bed in the nearest sleep-out and followed her husband across to the kitchen. She fetched down a large mug and made a fresh pot of tea.

"How much bread have we got?" he asked in the clipped tone of voice Margaret had become used to when his temper was fairly up.

"Not much, but I've more in the making. Why?" She answered

"Well we'll need some to take with us onto the fire" he said.

"What about meat?" She told him this was low too.

"So, how come we're out?" he asked

"Well George" his wife began, with as much patience as she could muster.

"This fire got up several days ago, towards the Leprosarium and Number One way and all the natives said they had to go. They asked me if I'd take them in the car and I said 'no I couldn't drive' and anyway I didn't want to be caught in the smoke with the baby. So they said they'd go. So I gave them bread and meat in a bag" she paused to look at George before continuing

"Then the men going through from K.D. with the cattle called in. They said they were out of bread and meat - so I gave them some as well. They used the phone too, to let the butcher know they were coming through." George continued to look like thunder 'Oh well, I might as well tell him it all at once' Margaret thought, 'he'll find out soon enough anyway' she plunged on bravely

"And I've only had Topsy and Roslyn to help me since the others left. They were supposed to be doing the watering. Instead of that they were eating a case full of fruit that I had in the sitting room. George I've been so busy I never noticed what they were up to."

Her husband glowered at her over the table. He swallowed the rest of his tea and with a sigh of profound exasperation, pushed his chair back and left the building.

'Oh dear,' thought Margaret 'He doesn't seem very pleased with the way I've been running things while he's been away.'

CHAPTER THIRTEEN

Home to Guyra

1944 – 1945

Another 'Wet Season' was approaching, the days hot and humid, the evenings sultry and still. Billowing white cumulo nimbus clouds built up beyond Napier Downs Station each night and Margaret felt more drained than usual.

John was eighteen months old. He had been a robust baby and until recently an active toddler, lurching along on sturdy chubby legs in the wake of his mother as she moved about the homestead. But now John had developed severe diarrhoea and Margaret was beside herself with worry as to the cause. She had always been a stickler for cleanliness, keeping all her son's belongings neatly on a table with a flycover spread over them. She made sure the verandah floor on which he played was mopped out daily with disinfectant and she boiled all his drinking water thoroughly. The mopping of the verandah became quite a daily ritual, with Margaret herself adding a good slosh of disinfectant to the bucket of water, ensuring that the native girls washed right into the corners of the room and then worked backwards to the door, so as to mop across their own footmarks.

Since John became ill Margaret had taken to keeping him up on the double bed, to be sure he could not pick up any more germs, and despite his listlessness, she found caring for him in this way tiresome and exhausting.

She had been minding him in this manner for some time, whilst still insisting on the daily disinfecting of the floors. Lying on the bed one day with her son, she chanced to notice that the vines were dying on the trellis outside the sleep-out. They were watered regularly and she puzzled over the cause as she lay idly playing with John during the noon siesta.

Several days later, whilst folding some linen, she heard Dora toss out a bucket of water into the garden. Leaving the neat pile of sheets on the bed Margaret went out to the steps.

"What was that Dora?" she called out to the girl below.

"What Missus? I just bin chuck'im dat ploor water out." She answered. "You're supposed to put it down the drain Dora. You'll burn the plants doing that with the sun on them." she remonstrated as she walked down the few steps into the garden. Evidence of the soapy suds still showed on the leaves of the Mexican rose which was looking sadly brown and withered, but Margaret's attention was drawn not to the sick looking vine but to the trail of dead grass running up to the base of the creeper.

"How long have you been doing this Dora?" she asked

"I bin do 'im dis way little bit long time Missus" The girl responded

"More quicker dis way" she added.

As Margaret stood and looked at the singed grass she was suddenly struck by a terrible idea.

She hurried round the outside of the house to the ablution block where the drum of disinfectant was kept under the concrete sink in the laundry. Bending down she pulled it out into the light. The label was old and all but illegible, the only words clearly decipherable were Sheep Dip in bold print and some of its chemical make-up. Of these just one sprang out to the horrified young mother. Arsenic. Margaret could not believe her eyes. She checked again. It could be nothing else. She had been disinfecting the floors with poison. No wonder poor little John was so unwell, yet this was the same drum, she was sure, that Mrs Smith had told her she used for cleaning purposes, there were still several of them left stacked at the back of the garage. She would get onto George right away about it, and have them moved and would make sure that a safe disinfectant was used in future.

Margaret was greatly shocked over the incident, although John's health slowly improved over the following weeks. She now decided the time had come to wean her son, as she herself felt more lethargic than usual. This would probably have been done sooner if she had not felt that breast feeding was the surest and safest way of nourishing John while he was ill. She now began the difficult task of introducing him to boiled goats' milk and solids in the form of mashed vegetables.

George had engaged the services of a station cook for the season, one Jim Rolleston from Queensland. His arrival had eased the burden for Margaret considerably, giving her more time for other duties and the caring of John.

Jim was a good cook, as station cooks go, but once ensconced in the kitchen he fiercely guarded his domain. Margaret found she could not easily use the kitchen to prepare meals for herself and George to take back to the privacy of their small flywired dining area, or boil and mash potatoes and pumpkin for John. Invariably, when she endeavoured to do so, the obliging cook insisted on performing these tasks himself. He then kept her waiting an in-ordinately long time to produce the food, which he liberally laced with black pepper, making it totally unsuitable for a finicky infant.

Margaret's exasperation grew. She felt the toll of the previous fourteen months had depleted her resources to a level she could barely endure. She did not know why she was so run down. Was it the burden of early motherhood, the lack of fresh fruit and vegetables or simply the stresses and strains of station life in an uncompromising climate? Whatever the cause she resolved to do something about it.

The mustering season was drawing to a close, the days were hot, the billabong little more than a muddy waterhole. Outside the homestead the vegetable garden was dry and dead, only the straggling remains of the last tomato bushes showed where the winter garden had been. Gusty afternoon winds whipped up clouds of dust from the bare, dry paddocks surrounding the homestead and finches in their thousands flocked to the water trough daily to sate their thirst.

"This is an unforgiving season, George" Margaret told her husband one evening, as they sat over their evening meal.

"Have you noticed how many birds have come to the billabong recently?"

"Yes Margaret. Most of the other waterholes have dried up. There must be thousands of whistling duck down there now. Did you see the pelicans come over this evening?" he asked.

George was a great lover of birdlife. He was constantly harranguing the piccaninnies out with their shanghais and was never too busy to stop and rescue some wet dishevelled bird caught in the top of a water tank. Margaret considered this love of wildlife and gentle handling of small suffering creatures to be one of his most endearing features.

When I went down to the Claypan today I came across some bastards from town shooting duck" he continued.

"It makes me sick how they go for the poor devils. What harm are they doing anyone?" and he clicked his tongue, shaking his head slowly in the characteristic way he had when something was beyond his understanding and deeply disapproved of.

Margaret looked across at him. He was lean and hard, yet there was a caring tender streak in him.

"I've decided to go home to New South Wales George" she announced unexpectedly, surprising herself as much as her spouse.

"I feel I need rejuvenating."

George continued with his meal. Long minutes passed. Disturbed as he was he showed no sign of having heard Margaret's announcement.

"I feel I need a good rest" Margaret continued, having waited in vain for some response.

"And I want to show John to my family."

"How long are you going for?" George asked at last, his face showing nothing of the turmoil he was experiencing.

"Well, I think about six months perhaps" she told him.

'Good Lord. Six months! Wives don't take off for six months at a time, surely!' George thought as he sat pondering over the last of his meal.

"You can't just take off like this you know Margaret" he told her.

"It's war time. You have to have permission from the Defence Department to move anywhere."

"Then I'll get permission George" she responded flatly.

"But I am going. I've decided."

"Will you be back?" George finally brought himself to ask.

"Of course I'll be back. Don't be so silly. I'm in need of rejuvenation that's all. Mum's seventy now and I should go home and see her. Now, there's some rice and stewed apricots here for sweets if you want it. Shall I serve it?" and so saying the meal once more took on the normality to which they were accustomed.

Permission duly obtained from the Defence Department, Margaret was at last ready to leave Meda and take the rest she longed for so much. There had been no further objections to her going raised by George, other than a wistful remark about mustering at Rarriwell.

"There's one more round to be done out there before the season breaks, Margaret" he told her one evening as they lay sleepless on top of the sheets.

"It's dangerous 'devil devil' country. Holey ground, mostly black soil, a bit of a worry galloping horses over it."

***George Wells with his son John
at Meda station. 1944.***

Margaret, lying on her back gazing up at the flyscreened ceiling smiled to herself at the implied danger. 'Does he really think I'd put off going because he's mustering Rarriwell country, she thought. They lay in silence side by side, both lost in their own private thoughts.

Presently George stirred.

"Are you awake Margaret" he asked

"Mmm. Why?"

"Did you hear me?"

"Yes George, I did. But what do you expect me to say. It's your choice whether you muster out there or not. There's not much I can do about it. I won't be here."

"Righto," he responded impatiently. "When is it you leave?" he asked, as if to indicate how little thought he had given the matter.

"Three days time. Will you be able to run us in to the airport?" she asked

The three days had passed quickly. There seemed a thousand last minute things to be done, clothes found for John suitable for the cooler climate of New England, her own faithful coat dyed and warm pullovers brought out of mothballs to be aired on the line. When she climbed into the car, John in her arms, the bags safely stowed behind them, she felt none of the excited anticipation she had expected. She was tired and rundown and felt only inclined to rest her head against the back of the leather seat and shut her mind to everything as George drove along the bumpy narrow track towards town.

The first leg of her flight took her from Derby up to the small Northern Territory town of Katherine where they stayed overnight at the AIM hospital. This building had been commandeered as quarters for the airforce. Margaret and her fellow passengers shared the accommodation with servicemen stationed in the region. Stretcher beds and blankets were supplied, but no sheets. John was without a cot for the first time in his short life, so Margaret laid him on a stretcher bed alongside her own, telling him to keep still. It was a good deal later that she thankfully saw his heavy, long lashed eyelids close, so that she too was able to go to sleep.

They flew from Katherine the following morning as far as Daly Waters. Here they met with near disaster. Shortly after take off, with seven passengers on board, oil spewed back across the windows of the little Avro Ansen plane, forcing the pilot to turn back and make an emergency landing.

Having drawn to a standstill on the station airstrip the passengers disembarked from the crippled aircraft. They watched in some surprise as the pilot alighted, his face as white as a sheet. From the excited conversation that erupted after the incident it soon became clear to Margaret how lucky they had all been. Bringing the small aeroplane round on its final approach the pilot had lost altitude, skimming alarmingly close to a fence line which he had only managed to clear by a few inches.

They were delayed at the small outpost of Daly Waters for two days, whilst a mechanic was sent down from Darwin to carry out the necessary repairs.

Their next stop, now two days behind schedule, was Charters Towers where they found the town celebrating it's annual race round. They landed late in the afternoon and were due to depart for Brisbane the following morning. Margaret and baby John were accommodated at one of the town's hotels, but they had to go to a different hotel for their meals. With them was a frail old lady, suffering from diabetes, who seemed to Margaret to be having difficulty travelling alone.

Northern Queensland was hot. Margaret, who had been carrying boiled water with her to keep John properly hydrated, wasted no time in getting her supply replenished. At the hotel the obliging staff filled a large gin bottle for her and she carried this wherever she went.

Having freshened up and finding there was still a little time before they were due at the other hotel for an evening meal, Margaret suggested a short walk to the elderly lady.

"We are not due for dinner just yet but we could have a little look around first. It's rather close inside and I feel I need some exercise after being cramped in that plane."

"Why, that would be very nice" her companion replied

"Only I am rather slow I'm afraid, and a bit lame."

Margaret smiled, "Don't worry, I don't intend to go far. I'm not a great one for walking you know, but I do think it might do us both good and we should sleep a bit better for it."

She helped the old lady to her feet and securing her hat firmly on her head, lifted John onto her hip, collected her handbag and the water bottle and led the way out of the room.

It was an interesting little excursion and not without humour. They saw several race goers, somewhat the worse for wear, lounging about aimlessly. With hats pushed back and wide grins on their florid faces the men had watched the trio with interest. Margaret, with her elderly companion leaning heavily on one arm and John hitched on her opposite hip, carried the gin bottle in her free hand. They were the object of much mirth amongst the onlookers, who whistled and yakkied loudly as they passed. Even for Margaret, a confirmed teetotaller and renowned for her sense of propriety, the humour of the spectacle they created was not lost.

The flight across to Brisbane the following morning was uneventful and Margaret was met at the airport by George's aunt, Nan. Nan Poole was Martha's younger sister who, being unmarried, had always taken a great interest in her older sister's offspring. Delighted now to greet her eldest nephew's wife and son Margaret found herself enfolded in a warm embrace of genuine affection. It was a week since she had left Meda and it's burdens behind her, but travelling with an active toddler was exhausting and it was with a sense of relief that she allowed herself to be gathered into the warmth of Nan Poole's hospitality.

For Margaret this was a week of sheer joy. She found her husband's aunt quite charming. She had also been able to catch up with her brother Bill, who was then stationed in Brisbane, with whom she spent long hours recounting tales of station life, whilst he in turn gave her news of home.

"You're looking rather thin and drawn Marge" he told her as he prepared to return to his barracks.

"Try to fatten yourself up a bit while you're with Mum."

"I'll do my best Bill" she said, smiling affectionately at him.

"It seems odd you telling me what to do. I seem to remember it was always me trying to bring you into line, not the other way round."

"Well you're right there Marge." Bill laughed

"But while I'm at it, remember, next time you're travelling let your poor husband know where you are!"

"Now come on Bill" Margaret broke in.

"George told me he was going off to muster Rarriwell before the season broke. I didn't see the sense in sending him a telegram when I knew he wasn't going to be anywhere near the homestead for goodness knows how long."

This was the second time she had been scolded over her lack of communication, Nan having taken her to task earlier in the week. George had clearly thought better of going back to re-muster Big Springs and Rarriwell. Instead he had been anxiously waiting for news of Margaret. Nan had received several telegrams from him, poorly disguising his concern, and had ensured that Margaret sent him word of her safe arrival at the first possible moment.

"Do you think, Bill," Margaret asked as a thought suddenly struck her

"that George only told me that he was mustering Rarriwell in the hope that I would delay coming over here."

"Now how would I know a thing like that Marge?" Bill responded

"Remember none of us have met this husband of yours yet, but I hope when this war is over, you'll bring him across when he's no longer man-powered on the station,"

"I'll do my best Bill" she promised.

"He's a good man you know, but with a mind of his own and not easy to move off his beloved station."

"Now you take care and I'll give your love to Mum and Vee when I see them in a day or two"

The final leg of Margaret's journey home was undertaken by train. She stepped onto the platform at Guyra into the arms of her sister Vera.

Vera, who was in the army, was home on leave and together they made their way to Malpass Street. Passing through the familiar gate, where an almost forgotten scent of climbing roses transported Margaret back to girlhood, she looked up to see her mother standing serenely at the edge of the verandah.

Vera, who had happily carried John from the station, watched as her sister set down her bag and hurried the last few paces up the footpath. With arms outstretched Jemima enfolded her long lost daughter in a prolonged embrace, at last setting her back at arms length and critically surveying her face. Vera, meanwhile, waited patiently nearby with John until Jemima called to her.

"Bring him over here Vee for me to have a look at. My first grandchild, what a bonny young fellow you are" she said running her hand caressingly through his dark hair. Meanwhile John looked in wide eyed wonder at the sudden attention his small presence seemed to be causing.

The following weeks were a panacea of delight for Margaret. Her homecoming was all she had hoped it would be. The gentle, early summer sun shone on the small New England township with none of the ferocity of the North and the rolling hills seemed to enfold her in well remembered delight. Here the landscape was her friend, the soft climate her tonic, as wallowing in utter contentment she allowed herself to be enveloped by her gentle mother's affection. However Jemima was not as well as she outwardly appeared and it was not long before Margaret's trained eye detected that something was amiss. Once the dragging exhaustion had left her and she felt more herself, Margaret, never one to be self-centred for long, began to notice the tell tale signs of pain and discomfort in her parent.

"What's the matter mother?" she enquired as they walked home from Church one Sunday.

"You aren't comfortable are you?"

"Oh, it's nothing Marge." Jemima replied

"A touch of old age I expect. One gets these things at my time of life you know."

But Margaret was not to be put off. She had noticed how awkwardly her mother had sat on the hard wooden pew, kneeling gingerly on her hassock and failing to sing, with her usual bird like voice, the hymns she knew so well.

"Tell me Mum. You must look after yourself you know. It's only sensible. I can't stay here for more than a few months, and with Bill and Vee away you'll be living on your own again by Easter."

"Stop fussing Marge." Jemima chided.

"It's nothing great. I'll be all right."

Margaret, not wanting to upset her mother further let the matter drop. Changing the subject she pointed out a neighbour tieing up a trailing rose in the garden over the road and they crossed to exchange greetings.

Later that evening, somewhat to Margaret's surprise, Jemima re-opened the conversation. They were sitting on the timber verandah watching the last of the daylight fade into dusk when Jemima said unexpectedly.

"There is something wrong Marge, but it's rather personal. I don't really like to speak of it"

The two women sat talking in hushed voices, Jemima briefly describing her symptoms to her daughter, Margaret listening and later asking a few pertinent questions.

"It can be fixed nowadays you know Mum. You don't have to put up with it. Why not go and see the doctor and see if he can arrange for you to have the operation."

"Oh I don't know Marge. I'm not very happy about an operation." Jemima said doubtfully.

Margaret sat quietly for a few minutes letting the idea take hold, before adding

"You know, it would be a good idea to get it done now while I'm over here. Then I'll be able to look after things for you while you go in. This house won't have to be left empty, and I'll be here to look after you when you come home, if need be."

The good sense of this last remark was not lost on Jemima. She had never ventured far from Guyra, only making one sortie to Sydney in her whole life. She could not bear the thought of leaving her home in Malpass Street unattended, even for a short while. Perhaps Marge was right after all and she should get herself looked at now while her daughter was home.

"All right. Perhaps I should do as you say Marge. I am finding it rather troublesome I admit."

Jemima Coakes was admitted to Glen Innes hospital early in 1945. She was seventy years old. Having undergone surgery, complications subsequently developed. The complications of such severity as to put Jemima in fear of her life.

"I am dying" she told her daughter.

"You must take me home where I may pass away in peace."

Margaret was greatly disturbed by this unexpected turn of events. The operation had apparently been accomplished satisfactorily but the post operative nursing care had been inadequate. In this year of 1945 good nursing care was not always possible, the country having lost many of its young nurses to the war and essential medical supplies being scarce or unobtainable.

Margaret, on receiving Jemima's desperate plea, contacted her friend and colleague Muriel Hatfield, then in Sydney. Muriel who had left Fitzroy Crossing some years earlier with rheumatic fever was now fully recovered and delighted to come to Margaret's aid. Catching a train to Guyra at the earliest opportunity she arrived at Malpass Street to assume the care of John, now almost two years old, enabling Margaret to give her full attention to her ailing mother.

Jemima Coakes, bedridden and in a very low condition was carried onto the train at Glen Innes by ambulance officers. Accompanied by her daughter she travelled back to Guyra. A taxi was at the station to meet them, the driver again carrying the old lady from the train to the waiting vehicle.

Once at home Margaret assumed full nursing care of her mother. She was catheterised at home, instruments being sterilised in an old kerosene tin boiled over the open fire. Day and night Margaret saw to all her mothers needs, experiencing again the burden of heavy nursing care. Jemima made a slow but certain recovery. Muriel, a wonderful support to Margaret during this time, had John in fine fettle. Margaret was much heartened by the success of her efforts. Only poor George, left alone in the heat of the Kimberley had cause to reflect on the perversity of fate, that kept his wife away from him so long.

Margaret spent more than five months in New England, before returning on the Overlander train to Western Australia. She broke her journey in Perth for a few days, staying with her mother-in-law Martha at Nedlands then flying North to Derby with MacRobertson Miller Airlines.

She had been away for the entire wet season and found the country greatly altered. All about her was brilliant green, the spear grass six to eight feet tall through the pindan. The boabs, though still in full leaf were no longer flowering, but out across the usually scalded flats beyond the Claypan lay a sea of magenta and pink. Carpets of wild portulaca and tiny pink everlasting flowers interspersed with blue grey rice grass basked beneath a clear blue April sky. Insects of every description abounded. As George drove her home from the airport swarms of grasshoppers rose up in waves as they passed, many becoming enmeshed on the radiator grill or caught against the windscreen. Butterflies flitted from flower to flower seeking nectar, whilst others flew tandem above them in a tangled flurry of delicate wings. Higher still numerous dragonflies circled and weaved in aimless abandon.

"Looks like the wets over for this year Margaret" George indicated the larger insects circling over the paddock.

"When the dragonflies are out like this, it's a sure sign the rains all gone" he told her.

"The birds will be having a field day. Plenty of tucker about for them now." and he chuckled happily to himself.

He was feeling unusually exhilarated this morning. Delighted as he was to have Margaret safely restored to him his feeling of elation was not solely due to her return home. It was brought about by a combination of delights, commencing early that morning when he had risen to find a heavy dew lying across the lawn. Jewel like droplets outlined a perfectly constructed cobweb strung between the verandah creepers, which George had been careful not to disturb as he made his way out to the ablution block. It was quite marvellous how the little creatures engineered such perfection he found himself thinking as he soaped his face preparatory to shaving.

The whole world felt somehow different today. George had experienced other mornings like this during his life, but somehow these first days of the dry never lost their magical feel. Overnight the heat and humidity vanished. The dawn brought a cool change, dew softened and moistened every wispy blade of grass and outlined every petal and leaf. As he had driven towards town George had marveled at the condition of the stock grazing in the lush grass now growing on the run. Hides shining with good health, rumps well covered, he found it difficult to recall the poor sunken appearance and protruding hip bones of these same cattle six months ago. April was surely the best month of the year in the Kimberley. A season of mustering to look forward to, billabongs and waterholes replenished, paddocks lush and green. Even the birdlife were having a field-day with a bountiful larder of insects and a million acres of grass seed. George was happy. He was happy for the stock, happy for the wildlife and happy for himself. Margaret was home.

CHAPTER FOURTEEN

Second Baby

1945 – 1946

The latter part of the Kimberly year, when the heat becomes oppressive and constant, is known by many as the 'silly season' or 'suicide month'. The body seems forever assailed by one discomfort or another. It is a time when the smallest of scratches will fester, boils will ulcerate, and chafe and 'prickly heat' become constant companions to all but the most leathery skinned inhabitants. It is a time when tormented minds cease to function rationally, anxiety levels peak and panic has a party. It is the time when people go 'troppo'.

Margaret was feeling in a precarious state. With one of the soundest minds, and more resilient natures, she was surprised at her own physical and mental frailty at this time. She was not in the habit of raising her voice, nor letting anyone break her calm exterior whatever the provocation, but one occasion caused her to do both.

Ted McKean was a donkey driver on Meda. He was a very good donkey driver, highly thought of by George, who had brought him down from Cherrabun soon after their move. He was, however, not on good terms with Margaret. He had not forgotten the manner in which, as a new bride, she had removed him from his room in the Old Cherrabun homestead to the less salubrious quarters next to the store-room. He was also irritated by her abhorrence of alcohol, knowing full well that she was aware of the tales about his days as a carter for the hotel. It used to take him three weeks, with two donkey teams, to carry the liquor supply through to Fitzroy Crossing and he often drank a good part of the consignment on the way. On one occasion, when intoxicated, his native partner Ella, a remarkable woman in Margaret's view, had placed him in the bell bag beneath the wagon and proceeded to drive both donkey teams, single-handed, the rest of the way.

Despite the low opinion Ted and Margaret had of each other it did not prevent him seeking her assistance in curing his 'sandy blight' and always the good practical nurse Margaret diligently administered black Argyrol drops until he was cured. A shrewd man, Ted now decided, during these long hot days at the tail end of the season, to teach 'the Missus' a lesson. She had been too firm and blunt for his liking and had lately been less well tempered than usual.

Ted was well pleased with his work as he took his place at the lunch table. He had been up to the Pindan Paddock close to the homestead and shot some wild donkeys during the morning. He had left them as they had fallen, carrion for the numerous kite-hawks which, even now, were wheeling above the dead animals. They would rot quickly enough he reasoned. The heat was intense, the flies prolific and, if the breeze held in its present quarter, the fragrance he anticipated from the gas swollen bellies and rotting flesh should soon be wafting nicely over the Meda homestead.

Margaret was three months pregnant. She was sick day and night and suffering from frequent migraines. She felt wretched. The weather was at its worst, the donkey wagon man at his most perverse, the natives needed more than usual nursing with a spate of infected sores and George seemed to be suffering from his annual end of season blues. Only John, now nearly two and half, seemed to be in fine form. This added to Margaret's misery as she tried to find enough energy to mind him.

Now there was a new irritation, Margaret had tolerated the stench as long as she could. Surely, she thought, George must have noticed it too. Each night as she lay down to sleep the cooling breeze she so longed for brought with it the unmistakable smell of stinking carrion. This aggravated the nausea from which she was already suffering. At night she kept a basin beside her in readiness, a towel and damp flannel lay on the upturned tea chest that was her bedside table.

"I've fairly had enough of that smell" she said to George as she returned with the rinsed out basin to the sleep-out.

"I won't put up with it any longer."

"If you don't burn those carcasses or get them shifted right away from here I shall leave. And I won't be back, George." She added as she recalled her last prolonged visit to Guyra. George, typically, did not respond to her outburst, but instead rolled over and went to sleep.

The following day a pall of thick black smoke rose into the hot October sky from the direction of Pindan Paddock. As Ted McKean put the finishing touches to the wagon he was working on a small but satisfied chuckle escaped him. 'I reckon that just about did the trick he mumbled quietly to himself. 'So the lady didn't like the perfume after all eh!' and he bent to resume his task.

At the conclusion of the war, life resumed a semblance of normality and for George and Margaret, who had perhaps been less inconvenienced than most, the freedom of movement was welcomed. George had been prevented from meeting any of Margaret's family having been man powered since before their marriage,

With the anticipated arrival of a new baby Margaret had invited her sister Vera to join her in Perth and return with her to Meda after her confinement. Remembering Margaret's difficult delivery of her first child, Vera had more than once indicated that she would like to be close at hand for any subsequent children Margaret and George might have.

In February Margaret was taken into Derby by George in the mule dray, as the road was flooded. From there she flew with John, then approaching his third birthday, to Perth and stayed once again with her mother-in-law, Martha, at Nedlands. Not seen by his grandmother since his birth, John was the subject of much interest to both the old lady and his Aunt Nora, who delighted in the antics of her young nephew. It was a happy time for the expectant mother. The cooler weather of Perth was refreshing, the company of her sister-in-law stimulating and with the anticipation of Vera's arrival and the new baby this was a happy time for Margaret. This state of affairs could not last. Margaret did not wish to jeopardize the tentative bond of friendship that was developing between her and her mother-in-law by encroaching on her hospitality for too long. Martha, whilst enjoying Margaret's company, was finding John increasingly tiring. In order to give Martha some much needed peace and quiet from her rolicksome grandson, Margaret arranged to spend a few days with Nora and her husband, Arch, at their Roleystone Orchard. They all greatly enjoyed this visit.

George Wells taking Margaret and John into Derby by mule dray to catch a plane to Perth before June was born. Native 'Frank' standing by. February 1946.

Soon after her return to Nedlands Margaret's concerns of tiring her mother-in-law were cut short. She went into labour unexpectedly early and before her sister's arrival in Western Australia. Martha saw her daughter-in-law safely admitted to hospital and wasted no time returning John to Nora at Roleystone. She told Margaret he would be much better cared for away from the city where there was an abundance of fresh fruit for him to eat and ample room to run free.

Margaret was delivered of a daughter, June Rosemary, on April 16th 1946. As blond as her brother was dark, with cherubic curls, dimples and large blue eyes she became a delight to behold.

The memories of John's birth almost three years ago flooded back to Margaret with the scent of hospital disinfectant and the crisp starched rustle of uniformed nurses and their hurried squeaking shoes. She recalled the loneliness she had felt then when no-one had visited her for days and lay now eagerly anticipating Vera's arrival.

Vera Coakes arrived in Perth on the Trans train and was met by Archibald Douglas, Margaret's brother-in-law. She was informed of her sister's admission to the King Edward Memorial Hospital, her niece's early arrival and Martha's need for some rest. Her bags were placed in the back of the waiting vehicle and she was driven away from the city toward the Darling Ranges up to the Roleystone orchard. Here Vera was met by Nora, who holding John securely by the hand, greeted her warmly and welcomed her into their home. Margaret meanwhile rested in her hospital bed, somewhat vexed and lonely.

In due course she was discharged and together with baby June stayed once more at Nedlands. Martha who was happy to enjoy some uninterrupted time with her new grandaughter, was kind to Margaret. Vera was managing John ably up in the hills where a kind hearted Nora was doing all in her power to make them feel at ease and welcome in her home. The situation was all that Martha could wish for. However this was not so for Margaret. Chaffing to regain her independence she found the brief visits Nora was able to make to Nedlands, with Vera and John, most unsatisfactory. She longed to return north where she would again be in command. This she resolved to do at the first opportunity.

She flew North with Vera and the children some weeks after

June's birth. The flight, although less gruelling than that previously undertaken by Margaret during the war with John, was not without incident. As they were approaching a fuel stop at Anna Plains station, South of Broome and on the Eighty Mile beach, June quite suddenly stopped breathing. Alarmed at her baby's apnoea attack Margaret held her up and shook her. She was relieved when the infant gasped and again drew breath. When the small aircraft touched down on the station airstrip Margaret hastened to alight.

"You can't disembark here" she was told by the flight attendant.

"We are only re-fuelling. You can get off once we arrive in Broome."

"My baby is very unwell and must have fresh air" Margaret explained.

"It is fearfully hot in the plane and I will not risk missing this opportunity to give her some relief. I won't get in your way." and she walked quickly past before another word could be uttered.

Once re-fuelling was complete, Margaret re-boarded the plane and took her seat near Vera, whom she had left minding John. The remainder of their journey was accomplished without incident.

The party were met at Derby airport by George. As Margaret carried her tiny daughter across the short distance to where her husband waited she could not have guessed the effect this second child was to have on her normally austere spouse. Over the coming years the delight George found in his little girl, whom he would take about the station with him whenever possible, slowly but inexorably chinked away at his stern exterior to reveal a warm hearted father Margaret had all but given up hope of discovering.

Vera settled in well to the hectic daily schedule on Meda, proving of invaluable assistance to Margaret, who was busier now than ever before. What happy times these were for Margaret. After five long years of war she now had some female companionship and cheerful conversation after those times of loneliness at the homestead. Someone to understand the aggravations, someone to delight at John's little achievements or be alarmed at his frequent escapades. Love George as she did, Margaret still found it difficult to accept that nothing seemed to move her husband, nor interest him much, other than the welfare of his beloved cattle.

He was polite and courteous to his sister-in-law. Indeed he appeared to like having her about the place, but his one great passion in life was the station and it's stock, his one desire to look after the Emanuel's interests. It often seemed to Margaret that she and her children would always come second to this.

CHAPTER FIFTEEN

A Riding Accident
1946

Margaret and Vera had visitors. The road from Derby to the outlying stations of Kimberley Downs, Napier and beyond, ran right by the Meda homestead. Visitors were a common occurrence. George and the stockcamp were out at Rarriwell mustering and had been away for some time. The station had seemed strangely quiet of late, so on this occasion the visitors were welcome.

Margaret and Vera had been planning to make soap that morning. The weather was still a trifle warm, but supplies were running short and it was a long hot chore that could not be postponed much longer. However, news that Ron Woodland's wife and sister in law were on their way out to join him at Kimberly Downs and would be passing through with Dick De Clerc in a taxi, soon put pay to any idea of soap making. The visitors arrived and were settled on the verandah with the tea tray.

"So Jack Lee is on Napier Downs now is he?" Margaret enquired

"And you're on Kimberley Downs. I understand there is quite a pleasant homestead there. I haven't been myself, but George has spoken about the place often."

"George used to do the mail run in the 'wet season years ago, you know" she continued, putting the ladies at ease with her cheerful talk.

"He used to take three weeks to do the trip, with pack mules of course, from Derby right through to Mount House."

"Really. That's most interesting" murmured the ladies in unison,

"And how long ago did he do the mail run. It must have been quite a strenuous trip at that time of the year."

"Well yes, I suppose it was" Margaret agreed.

"George is a fine bushman you know, most capable. He was only a young man then. It was long before I met him. More tea?"

June, sleeping beneath a protective net at the far end of the verandah stirred in her sleep, making small baby noises that stilled the conversation for a moment. Vera crept across the timber boards to take a peep at her, Mrs Woodlands following.

"Oh, but she's gorgeous" the visitor whispered.

"How old is she now did you say?"

"Five weeks." responded the proud aunt "and a good baby too thank goodness. Poor Margaret has her hands full here you know, so we're lucky to have an easy child."

Across the lawn the native girl Roslyn, Willie Lennard's young wife, was minding John. The three year old boy was teasing the slender Aborigine with a 'shakey paw' lizard he'd found and there was much happy giggling from both child and nursemaid. Vera and her guest returned to join the tea drinkers.

It was mid afternoon. The guests were preparing to take their leave when John ran to the gate with the native girl hot on his heels.

"Horse comin' Missus" Roslyn turned toward Margaret.

"Horse comin'" echoed John cheerfully.

"Daddy, daddy comin'"

Margaret stepped quickly down into the garden and along the path. A native stockboy rode towards her and dismounted. He looked excessively weary, dusty and dishevelled. His eyes were bloodshot and his manner agitated.

"It's 'Boss', Missus. 'im had a fall. 'is leg Missus... You come."

The native boy pointed distractedly into the distance.

"The boss has had a fall?" echoed Margaret, trying to grasp what the boy was saying.

"Yes Missus. You come Missus" he nodded his head rapidly at her.

"His leg, it all dis way, no good Missus" he told her.

" When did he have the fall?" Margaret asked

The stockman looked puzzled. He stood quiet for a moment, then pointing to the sky indicated where the sun would have been at about ten o'clock in the morning. It was now nearly three in the afternoon.

"What is it?" Vera questioned Margaret as she joined her sister.

"Has there been an accident?"

"Yes Vee. Apparently it's George. He's taken a fall and I think it must have happened some hours ago. They're out at Rarriwell you know. It's a long way out and it's taken this boy many hours to ride in here. He's made good time if it's as far as I think. I've never been there."

"Oh Dear" Vera looked deeply concerned.

"What's to be done?"

"Well, I must go out to him." Margaret told her.

Mrs Woodlands, joining the group, overheard the latter part of the conversation.

"Look Margaret, Dick De Clerc can drive you out in the taxi. That's the best thing." she said decisively

"Yes. Thank you. Vera, you must mind the baby here while I'm gone. Roslyn will look after John." Margaret soon took a hold of herself.

"But what will I do to feed the baby?" Vera asked anxiously, for June was still wholly breast fed.

"Give her some boiled water" Margaret said shortly

"But what if she cries" Vera persisted.

"Then let her cry, Vee. She's not going to die, and I will be back sometime."

"Will you ring us from along the way?"

"Vera! " Margaret looked at her sister sternly.

"There are no phones out there! It's about twenty-five miles of bumpy station track. If there was a phone along the way someone would have rung us, not ridden five or six hours on horseback!" and so saying she excused herself abruptly and gathered together some bandages, morphia and brandy. She arranged for some bags of flour to be loaded into the taxi, to weigh the vehicle down and lessen the jolting for the return journey, and smartly discouraged the station cook from any idea of accompanying her. With as little loss of time as possible Margaret gathered her wits about her, dispelled all thoughts of a negative nature and urged Dick De Clerc to set forth whilst they still had daylight enough to find their way.

They headed out from the homestead in an easterly direction, soon taking a sharp turn north across the May River towards Yuringa. Somewhere between No. 4 and Daley's bore they struck a sharp rut in the road and Dick De Clerc felt the steering break.

"Where's there a fence round here?" he asked Margaret

"I need a piece of wire."

"I have no idea" she told him. This was not very helpful she knew, but George had always been reluctant to take her driving about the station, so she was naturally unfamiliar with the landscape.

"Well I'll take a look in the back of the car. We might have a billy can there," he said. This he found and swiftly removed the handle to wire up the steering.

Presently they were able to continue on their way, although the loss of time had been of some concern to Margaret who was still trying to rid herself of images of George lying injured miles from anywhere. A swift silent prayer eased her mind and she cast her thoughts to the more practical aspects of the situation.

A Riding Accident

George was annoyed. He had spent most of his life in the saddle and knew himself to be a fine horseman. He was a careful, practical man, rarely impulsive and always conscious of potential dangers. His vision and foresight was second to none, yet here he was lying on the ground with a broken leg.

He was suffering intolerable pain, particularly when seized by muscle spasms which dispelled all else, his anger included. The shock he had experienced after his fall was slowly passing. He felt as if he had been propped up here for a lifetime with his leg on a couple of bags of hobble straps. How it hurt. How it bloody well hurt. He was not a swearing man, but he felt like swearing now. This was a mess and no mistake. How long would it take that boy to ride in, he wondered. Would he do as he should and cut across country? Yes he probably would. That was why they'd sent him. He knew his way about. It was almost uncanny how well he knew his way. But would he ride sensibly. No use taking it too fast. The horse wouldn't make the distance if he did. He must just go 'steady, steady' and hopefully he would make the station before nightfall.

He wondered who'd come out to fetch him in. He was hoping Margaret might come, but it was unlikely. She was too damned concerned about her babies. He remembered how she'd fussed over taking John down to a bushfire because of the smoke, and John had been a deal older than June was now.

What time was it? Time was passing so slowly. Still, the sun was almost down. A shiver ran through him, followed the same instant by a spasm of excruciating pain. One of the men put a saddle cloth over him. That felt nice. The horse smell was comforting. He closed his eyes.

He didn't sleep. What an impossible thought, but the shock had had an effect on him that left him weary beyond belief. Darkness fell and time passed. The night noises of the bush went unheeded until presently he felt, rather than heard, the distant throb of a motor.

At first, barely daring to believe his senses, the sound little more than a vibration in the still night, discernible only to one accustomed to the silence of the bush, it grew in intensity until it could no longer be doubted. For doubt it, George did. He felt decidedly strange and was fearful that his physical torment was playing tricks on his mind.

Presently a pale light touched the tops of the wattle scrub, followed a short time later by a clear glimpse of headlamps through the close growing timber. George stirred himself. He ran a rough hand over his face and re-adjusted his hat more comfortably on his balding head. He watched as Margaret clambered out of the vehicle clutching various packages. She strode briskly toward where he lay.

"Here take this" she said giving him a few drops of brandy she'd poured onto a spoon.

"It'll make you feel better. Then I'll take a look at you." She screwed the lid back on the bottle and surveyed him, for all the world as if she were nursing any patient in any hospital ward.

Seized with stomach cramps George had barely swallowed the firey liquid than he vomited painfully but thoroughly at her feet. She stepped back briskly.

"This won't cure me Margaret" he said crossly when he recovered.

"I've broken my leg."

"Yes George, I can see that" Margaret answered him patiently.

"Now I'm going to administer some morphia. It should ease the pain a little, then I'll try to splint the leg so we can move you." She was calm and professional. Uncannily so it seemed to the small group of stockmen watching the proceedings from a discreet distance.

Presently, when Margaret judged the drug to have taken some effect, she set about splinting the broken limb with newspaper and boards. George was in terrible pain. His wife gave him another sixth of morphia, praying it wouldn't harm him. With assistance from a couple of the men she proceeded with the splinting again, bandaging it firmly in place to immobilize the broken bones.

Moving George to the car was the greatest ordeal of all. He

was hugely strong and a powerfully built man. Carrying him to the vehicle and easing him in was a difficult task, but accomplished without mishap. Dick De Clerc climbed into the drivers seat and gingerly set the car in motion.

The ground was rough black soil country, pitted with holes and hardened hoof prints. It was criss crossed with cattle pads and scattered with hard tussocks of Mitchell grass. It was impossible to drive smoothly. Every bump and lurch was felt by the occupants, excruciatingly so by Meda's manager. It was a slow journey back to the homestead, which they did not reach until nearly midnight. They had been forced to pull up many times along the way to give George a rest from the painful jarring and once to administer a further dose of morphia. It was a relieved party that finally drew up alongside the homestead.

Once there Margaret told George that she had telephoned Dr Hertz earlier to tell him what had happened and that he would be waiting in Rowell's office to hear from them.

"I'm NOT going into town now Margaret" George told her.

"I'm filthy dirty from the camp. They'll keep me in hospital, and I need to see that things are in order here before I go."

"See to what things George?" Margaret enquired.

"I can clean you up a bit first, so don't worry about that,"

"No. I'm not going in. I need to make sure things are locked up and that the books are in order. I can't go in tonight. I must see everything's right, it's my job, Margaret."

His wife, knowing this tone well, knew better than to argue. He wasn't in too bad a way if he felt up to taking this line. He had not sustained a compound fracture and it was already too late to worry about setting the leg before the swelling took place. More than twelve hours had elapsed since his fall, so his leg was already very swollen indeed. She conveyed as much to Dr Hertz on the phone a short time later and was relieved when he agreed to allow George to remain at the station overnight. It would be another long slow and arduous journey in to Derby. It would be better for the patient to get some rest first and tackle the drive in daylight.

The next day Margaret had taken George into the hospital at Derby. She took baby June with her, leaving Vera to mind John on the station. A few spare nappies were stuffed into a bag, together with personal items necessary for George's inevitable stay in hospital. Margaret, too pre-occupied to consider her own requirements, had taken no change of clothes for herself. This lapse had been sharply brought home to her when the baby messed all over her dress during the drive in. Margaret tolerated this indignity until they reached Derby, when she retired to a bathroom, removed and washed the offending garment, then wore it soaking wet to dry in the cool May sunshine.

George, as expected, was admitted to Derby Hospital where he remained a patient for some days. Emanuel Brothers, having been informed of the accident, were most anxious to do all they could for the family. Apart from arranging for Dan Luck to fly North without delay to take over the reins on Meda, they also urged Margaret to allow them to have George transferred to Perth for whatever medical attention proved necessary. Margaret knew that the death of George Poole, her husband's late uncle from GoGo, must still weigh on the minds of those in Head Office. Whereas Gordon Smith, George's predecessor, had been beyond help, in the current situation clearly something could be done to avoid any unnecessary complications.

Despite Emanuel's well meaning offers, however, George remained in Derby. He had no wish to be moved further away from his beloved station, but continued to fret and sulk even where he was. He was proving a cantankerous patient and it was decided to discharge him at the earliest possible moment into the care of his wife, who was known to be a very capable nurse. George came home to Meda to convalesce and await full recovery.

He was not an easy patient, Margaret decided, as she removed the tattered cover from the pillow on which he rested his injured leg and replaced it with a new one. This was the fourteenth he had spoiled with his chaffing. It grieved her to see him agitatedly moving his leg, heavy in its plaster cast, from side to side.

"Can't you do something to stop this cursed itching?" He demanded for the umpteenth time that morning.

"Did you try the ruler I left on the bedside table George?" She asked as she placed June down in the meat safe cot for her daily nap.

"It's not long enough." he grumbled, sliding his leg from side to side in a useless attempt to ease the itch. Margaret watched him for a moment. The new pillow slip was already heading the same way as the previous dozen.

"I'll see if I can find something George" she told him.

"I won't be long. Do you need some more water in your jug?" she enquired before she left the sleep-out.

She returned a few minutes later carrying a jar and a spoon.

"I'm just going to put a little methylated spirits down the gap inside of the plaster for you George" she told him, as she poured a small amount of the clear liquid onto the spoon.

"Now hold still while I try to get it in." It proved quite difficult to get the liquid to flow to the bottom of the plaster. The cotton wool absorbed much of it and the small gap between plaster and flesh made it awkward to get in. Margaret did not want to use too much, in case the liquid damaged the cast, so she was sparing but persistent.

Eventually success was achieved.

"Good God! It stings Margaret!" George exploded a moment later.

"What have you done, dammit? It's burning me." and he shot a thunderous look at his wife who stood helplessly by his bedside.

George, after his initial outburst, was speechless, but the agitated thrashing against the pillow intensified. His face was dark with rage.

It was obvious to his poor wife that she had made a severe error of judgement. Far from soothing an itch, she had aggravated and inflamed the leg to a far greater degree of discomfort than before. Worse still, there was no way she could undo the damage. George must endure the pain as best he could until 'The White Lady' evaporated.

The weeks passed slowly. The bones began to knit and George, always a conscientious and loyal employee, felt bound to get up and about as soon as he was able.

"Emanuels are still paying me Margaret" he told his wife when she urged him to remain resting a little longer.

"I'll be quite all right. Stop your worrying. It's time I earned my keep."

"But George, surely you don't need to be down there cementing that septic!" She protested.

"There are others who could do that work. We've lived this long with a bucket toilet, I'm sure a few more months won't do us any harm."

Her husband looked at her. She thought he was going to respond, but, as was usually his way, he merely gathered his hat and stick and made his way awkwardly down the steps and across to the newly dug septic without another word.

Margaret and Vera had spent the morning making a batch of soap. A job they had delayed since the day of George's fall. Fat from the killers had been saved, rendered down and strained in advance. Using the clean fat, water, resin and caustic soda the two sisters, with help from Dora and Ngungala, had poured the mixture into large tubs to set. When it was set they would cut it up and store it on shelves to dry.

Although Margaret did not use the station soap for personal use, it proved handy for washing dishes out in the stockcamp, for homestead laundry and any other cleaning jobs about the place. It was rough and harsh, drying into hard cracked unattractive cakes, but was a good addition to the limited supplies available for general hygiene.

"What a lot of work there is to be done" Vera said to her elder sister as they placed the last tub to set.

"I never quite realised how full your days were until I came to stay. Doesn't George ever take you out on the run for a bit of a spell and a look around?"

"Oh he does from time to time Vee." Margaret said

"Though he doesn't really like to. I remember one time about a year ago when he took me. John was two and we went out to a place called Number Six to pull the bore. The native, Brandy, used to camp out there minding the bore and pumping water for the cattle when needed."

"Who's Brandy?" asked Vera "Have I met him?"

"I don't think so Vee. He's an elderly aborigine who doesn't come into the homestead very often. Proper gentlemanly he is."

"Anyway, George worked on the bore. It was getting late and he decided he wouldn't return to the station. He worked well into the night."

"But you said you had John with you Marge." Vera interrupted.

"Yes, I know. George is like that. He wasn't going to waste Emanuel's fuel driving us home. We had a bit of salt meat and damper with us, so we stayed."

"Anyway, as I said, George worked into the night and I put John to sleep on his bunny rug in the back of the truck. I was a bit afraid he might wake and fall out. But he didn't. I didn't know where I was going to sleep. I was feeling fairly done I can tell you." Margaret sighed at the memory.

"You can have my bed Missus', Brandy told me. 'Not likely' I was thinking to myself. Not being disrespectful or anything Vee, but can you imagine. Him camped out there all through the 'Dry' and the state the bed would be in."

"So what did you do Marge?" Vera looked with wonder at her sister.

"No, no Brandy. It's all right, I'll sit in the truck", I told him. 'You come an' look 'im Missus' he said to me.

'I put fresh bags on.' Anyway Vera, he had two corn sacks and four or six forked stakes. A rail was pushed either side of the bags and it was suspended like a hammock. So I slept in this set up, and Vee, it was the most comfortable bed I've had in my life. He was such a gentleman and treated me with courtesy. So what do you think about that." She finished with a flourish.

"And that was the end of your trips out with George was it?" Vera laughed.

"Oh well he did take me sometimes if it was only for a short run." Margaret told her.

"But you know Vee, he'd drive to a bore and we'd sit. Just sit. I couldn't believe it. I'd ask him what we were doing and he'd say 'I just want to see such and such a cow, or such and such a bullock'. We'd be there for hours and it fairly drove me!" She ended, raising her eyes in a look of mock exasperation.

The two sisters laughed together happily.

"But this won't do" Margaret sighed.

"Look at the time. We must get a move on or we'll never get done by lunch." and they hurried about their business once again.

CHAPTER SIXTEEN

Vera

1946 – 1947

It was September 1946. Those first days of what in other parts of the country would be called Spring, here in the tropics still ' The Dry', but with a subtle change in the air. Over the past few weeks humidity levels had increased, the dry winds had ceased and a warm stillness enveloped the station.

The bauhinias, heavy with crimson pods, were showing the first traces of delicately tinted new leaf growth, the bountiful feast of nectar laden flowers spent for another year. Birdlife was evident in every tree and shrub in Margaret's garden. Friar birds and miners chattered and sang, jostling for position, suspended in the burgeoning boughs where they fed. Numerous black heart and zebra finches flocked about the water troughs. Down on the billabong spoonbills, ibis, stilts and whistling duck by the thousand, eeked out a living from the ever diminishing food supply to be found there. The ducks, Margaret thought, were reaching plague numbers. Something would have to be done about them.

"Go down to the billabong and catch some of those ducks" Margaret told the native girls.

"There are so many of them there now, there's hardly space for them to land."

"Oh no Missus!" Daisy and Dora looked fearfully at Margaret. "We can't do dat. The boss he won't like it. He looks after 'dem birds Missus. We can't kill 'em those ones."

Janet Wells

"Nonsense!" Margaret responded. "They need thinning out, and anyway the boss isn't here. So off you go. They'll be good tucker."

Margaret liked the birds. She was well aware that George did too, but he was ridiculously fond of them. He had protected them ever since he had come to Meda over three years ago. It was time something was done about them. Sensible is sensible, Margaret thought, as she watched a small party from the camp head down to the water's edge some time later.

She watched, fascinated by the silent stealth of the hunters. They reached the water's edge causing barely a stir amongst the flock. One long necked crane rose from the muddy shore line, winging its way slowly and majestically across to the farther side of the billabong where it alighted elegantly on a dead limb. No other disturbance was evident to Margaret as she stood watching from the bottom of the homestead garden.

One or two of the natives had broken off leafy saplings or bushes and were crouching down behind these. With fronds of coolibah tied around their heads and wrists, they moved slowly and silently into the water. Creeping up on the unsuspecting birds they were able to get close enough to reach out and snatch them by the legs, pulling them swiftly and silently down under the water. One after another the ducks were pulled under, before any sound could escape them that would alarm the rest of the flock.

Presently, however, there was a sudden flurry of wings as the two elderly gins waded from the water. Their dark bare breasted bodies emerged wet and shiny, as they proudly held aloft their catch. There was much excited chattering and laughter from those who had remained concealed on dry land. Margaret watched as, in unison, thousands upon thousands of whistling duck rose in panic, wheeling high over the water, their agitated commotion reaching the ears of all at the homestead.

"Whatever's going on down there?" questioned Vera emerging from the kitchen with flour on her hands.

"Just the natives catching a few duck Vee. Don't let on to George mind, he's quite potty about them you know. But they need a bit of culling." Margaret told her sister.

"If only you knew what I have to put up with." She continued.

"George and his pets! We had a pet bullock once, it had been reared as a poddy in Gordon Smith's day. It was a big animal, Vee, and the most terrible nuisance. It used to climb up into the kitchen, walk in through the door and eat anything that was left about. Rolled oats, cabbage, anything. Even soap!"

"Gosh! I can't imagine you putting up with that Marge" Vera smiled at her sister's indignant expression.

"Well I didn't. I was all for getting rid of it, but George wouldn't get rid of it. It was his pet! Anyhow, it got down round the drovers who were camped at the billabong. You know the stock route goes by there. Something must have happened to it. I don't know if it was poisoned, bitten by a snake or what, but it died down there. George was terribly upset about it."

"You didn't have anything to do with that Marge, did you?" Vera asked her sister quizzically.

"Oh Heavens no! I wouldn't dare touch his precious cattle Vee. But a few wild duck, well that's quite different." Then changing the subject entirely she continued

"You will remember to save the potato peelings for a new yeast starter, won't you?"

Vera had decided to stay on Meda with her sister for the remainder of the season having been put on the books as Station Cook by George some months earlier. It had been a good move in Margaret's opinion, for life had been running much more smoothly with a little co-operation and companionship from the kitchen. She had endured various cooks, some capable but difficult, others lamentable. Vera's predecessor had made the most shocking bread ever seen by Margaret. "It's nothing but sods!" she had complained to George who could not help but agree, and so Vera had been given the job instead.

She was a good cook, capable and hard working. But of more importance to Margaret than this was the fact that she was impeccably clean. Margaret no longer had to watch that the floors were mopped daily, the meat kept covered, the fly cloth placed over the milk or the dishes washed in scalding water. She was left free to attend to the numerous other matters that constantly presented themselves for her attention.

Only last week, in the middle of the morning, they had carried Maudie up to her on a blanket from the camp. Maudie, who had been married to Long Nugget had become pregnant before his untimely death six months earlier, and was now in the final stages of labour. Margaret had delivered the baby, Alice, up at the house, tied the cord and handed the infant to its mother. There had been no complications, the after birth came away freely, the baby suckled well at her mother's breast and Margaret had been in no way disturbed by the event. It was part of the daily life on Meda at that time.

They had had a good season all round, Margaret considered. She felt rejuvenated in the company of her sister. The daily problems and niggling annoyances seemed to diminish in importance when discussed with Vera. George was so laconic by nature that Margaret found it difficult to get him to talk over anything with her. She would usually get a clipped "Yes" or a curt "No", but not much else, which she found was of little help when trying to air grievances or get annoyances off her chest. With Vera it was different and she felt happier. Margaret was also cheered by the additional company Vera attracted. Don Bowden, from Blina, had become quite a regular caller on his way to and from Derby and Margaret was encouraged to think that a discreet romance was in the air. Mr Bowden had even taken Vera into Derby with him once or twice, when her duties in the kitchen had not been too pressing. Margaret wondered whether George had noticed the friendship as well. He certainly had not mentioned it to her, but it would not be like him to do so.

Margaret wondered if Vera might end up marrying Don Bowden. She would then have her sister on the neighbouring station and family close at hand indefinitely. But fast on the heels of this thought came the realisation that Jemima would have lost both her precious daughters to the furthest corner of the continent. It was folly to wonder at the outcome in this way. The Lord would know what was best for them all, Margaret decided.

Emanuels would, through their agent in Derby, notify George of bullock numbers required for shipment, the dates to be met and so on. The stock camp worked feverishly to muster the required number of bullocks, which were later taken by drovers along the stock route to Yabbagoodie and so into the holding yards at Myalls Bore. Here they awaited further orders from the agent about loading times. The ships were loaded at low tide, the vessel sitting on the muddy bottom of the King Sound. George and his men drove the bullocks from Myall's Bore across the marsh behind the town of Derby, into the yards close by the jetty, down the long timber cattle race and onto the waiting vessel.

Margaret always felt immense relief at the completion of a successful live shipment. George became more relaxed. The tension of meeting deadlines lifted, he would allow himself a few days around the homestead, updating the station books, fixing engines and attending to minor maintenance about the place. Margaret enjoyed these times. She would wash and freshen his bed roll, launder his clothes and mend the inevitable rents in his work garments. Sometimes they would go together into Derby to collect fresh fruit and vegetables for the station. Although their main stores came up by ship twice a year and were delivered to them by Albert Archer, the carrier, Margaret also tried to keep up a regular supply of fresh goods for the inhabitants at Meda. She enjoyed her occasional visits to town, despite finding it aggravating to lose George to the hotel for longer than she liked. He was a hard working manager for Emanuels and totally abstemious at home, so she tried not to begrudge him a certain amount of ' good cheer' when the opportunity arose. On these occasions she would sit patiently, outside the hotel in the hot vehicle, sometimes for hours until George eventually emerged. Once they had attended a local wedding together, in town, meeting up with many of their friends. Margaret had enjoyed the occasion, but was surprised when George took her newly replenished glass from her saying,

"You've had enough Margaret."

"Don't be ridiculous George! It's me who tells you when you've had enough, not the other way around." She responded indignantly.

"Anyway, I'm only drinking squash" she added

"That isn't squash Margaret, it's alcoholic punch" he told her. Shocked to find she had unwittingly been consuming liquor, Margaret later admitted to having a 'very dry mouth' and to feeling as if she was 'going in the back legs'.

These happy times together were usually short-lived. Invariably George, after a few days, would roll his swag and head off once more to the stockcamp, where the cycle would begin all over again.

The culmination of the year, that had seen Vera's arrival in the Kimberley, baby June's birth and the installation of a modern septic system at the Meda homestead, was the official engagement of Don Bowden, manager of Blina Station, to Vera Coakes. George and Margaret Wells were quietly delighted. Don was considered by all to be a steady and reliable man. Vera, like her sister, was known to be capable and caring. The combined qualities of the two boded well for a long and rewarding marriage.

Vera, in love though she was, felt certain pangs of remorse. Her mother Jemima, so far away, was now losing her second daughter to the remoteness of the Kimberley. Vera, in the first month of the new year resolved to go home for an extended visit.

Her sister and future brother-in-law drove her, in very wet conditions to Derby. Here the local station agent was reluctantly persuaded to hand over a registered parcel addressed to Don Bowden that had arrived after the onset of heavy monsoonal rains. This contained an engagement ring which Don had been unable to present to Vera himself. She placed it securely on her finger and left the Kimberley to spend the next ten months with her mother in the cool climate of New England.

At the completion of mustering, in September 1947, Don Bowden travelled to New South Wales. He and Vera were married in the Hurstville Baptist Church, Sydney, on October 4th. In the congregation were Jemima Coakes and her son Bill. Margaret and George Wells sent a telegram to the couple from Derby.

After a short honeymoon the couple returned to the Kimberley by boat, so that Don could resume his position as manager of Blina. During the voyage all of their wedding gifts were stolen. Vera had to establish a home with only the barest essentials.

Their marriage proved to be a long and happy one and their first child, a son, born the following September, became the enticement that ultimately brought Jemima to the Kimberley.

CHAPTER SEVENTEEN

Jemima Visits

1948

Jemima was seventy-five when she decided to make the journey to Western Australia. The decision had not been taken lightly, for she was far from keen about travelling, but the separation from her two daughters was proving difficult to endure. She still had not met Margaret's husband nor seen her grand-daughter June. To add to her feeling of isolation Vera and Don were now expecting their first-born. The family was growing, yet she was becoming less a part of it. Margaret wrote regularly begging her to consider making the trip and so forceful was her style of writing it sometimes seemed as if she assumed her mother would do as she bid if the tone of her letters were strong enough.

Jemima was often amused by the forthright manner adopted by her eldest daughter. She frequently wondered about the nature of the unknown George and how he coped with Margaret's dictatorial ways. One of her letters, written in February, had been so presumptuous Jemima could not help but smile when she thought of it.

'My Dear Mum' she had written

'Received your long letter and am pleased you are keeping o.k. Yes I think you may as well sell the land if you can. Just keep what you say. Getting it fixed up while Bill is on holidays is a good idea too.

Now, I was wondering if you might go to Sydney

about the end of May and come over here by plane. It is three hours to Melbourne. Don's sister could meet you. Then it is one day from Melbourne to Perth. I could arrange for someone to meet you there and put you on the plane for Derby. That would be two whole days and three hours getting here by plane. You could stay till the end of December. You could perhaps come over the following winter if you liked it and see us both again.

At present am hoping we won't have to spend more than three years more up here. But it all depends on world conditions etc.

Your fare here by plane all the way would be about fifty pounds altogether. Twenty-eight pounds Sydney to Perth. Sixteen pounds, ten shillings Perth to Derby and your train fare from Guyra to Sydney. About fifty pounds I should say.

Think about it and if you get the business fixed while Bill is home and cleaned up by the end of May you could spend the winter in comfort and still have your corner to go back to.'

Having gone into such detail over the practical aspects of the journey and its estimated cost, the letter continued as if it were all settled.

'Put in a warm suit for travelling 'and bring a lot of summer frocks. Don't bring too much luggage. Thirty-five pounds allowed on the plane. One good sized suitcase and a small one would do.'

She had then let the matter rest for a page or so whilst she told of the children's health. Don's recent visit from Blina and what George was up to.

'He has to send the car engine away, so guess we will be without a car for three months at least.'

Jemima Coakes,
Margaret's mother, aged 74. 1947

The weather as always took up much of Margaret's page space, this time putting her in mind of another worthwhile instruction to her parent.

> *'Was thinking again about leaving one room locked. It would want to be a room without a fireplace, because you can imagine how it would rain down in the winter into the fireplace. We had rain eight days in succession. Four and a half inches one day, ten inches in the eight days. Killed a snake last night in the bathroom'*........

Jemima, getting on in years, had been considering selling off some of the land attached to 'Roslyn" and her other small house in Malpass Street. It was becoming too much for her to maintain and there seemed little point in keeping it. Her plans, however, were not as swiftly executed as Margaret had supposed. It was not until winter was well advanced that Jemima finally had her affairs settled to her satisfaction.

Vera, by this time nearing her confinement, was planning for a delivery in Derby Hospital, rather than making the long trip to Perth as her sister had done. Jemima, who had assisted at the birth of many of her nephews and nieces, was anxious to be of help to Vera. She finally plucked up the courage to leave New England and journey across the continent, as directed by Margaret, arriving in the Kimberley in August 1948.

George had come in from the stockcamp to meet her off the plane. Margaret and Vera were with him. Her son-in-law was tall and leaner than she had imagined and although courteous towards her, seemed unusually quiet and uncommunicative.

"Is he always so sparing with words?" she asked Margaret, during a quiet moment later that day.

"Yes he is Mum" Margaret told her.

"You know, people ring him at night, sometimes Jack Lee, the people at Kimberley Downs or the stock agent. They'll talk to George for up to half an hour and all he ever says is 'Yes' or 'No' in varying tones of voice. That's his whole contribution to the conversation. What they're telling him I've no idea! It's the funniest thing you've ever heard."

"But what about to you at home?" Jemima asked.

"He must talk to you about things."

"Not really Mum. I do most of the talking and he does all the listening!" she laughed merrily.

"But we rub along well enough." Suddenly remembering an occasion when she had pressed her laconic husband to state his feelings more, she added.

"You know, once I said to him 'you never tell me you love me George' and you know what he replied? He said ' Margaret, I told you I loved you before we were married and I haven't changed my mind! There is no mistake about him though, he can do nearly anything. Make saddles, bridles, anything in the blacksmiths' line. He's mended a clock with a broken spring for me and he can fix a car anywhere out in the bush." Jemima patted her daughter's arm affectionately.

"I'm sure he can," she said tolerantly.

"I'm glad you've found a good man Marge. You deserve it. Forever 'doing' for other people you are and I want you to be happy."

"Well I'm perfectly contented Mum, though there are times when I get exasperated. Because I'm a nurse George thinks I can work miracles. In cases of sickness he'll say 'but you're a nurse Margaret'. 'Yes' I'd say, 'but I'm not God and I haven't got the equipment to do anything with!' Sometimes I'm sure he thinks I'm fairly useless, but he's good to me all the same."

They sat up later than usual that first evening. Margaret glowing with the pleasure of this long awaited moment.

Vera, who had been brought down to Meda by Don the week before, had retired to bed early. She was to remain on the station with Margaret for the last month of her pregnancy and being heavy with child was weary from the day's excitement. George, likewise, had turned in soon after the supper dishes were cleared. He was to return to the stockcamp the following day and would be up, as always, long before sunrise. Margaret and Jemima had the verandah to themselves, their happy chatter merging with the night noises of the bush, long after the moon had risen above the stark contorted branches of the bare boab trees.

"Marge dear! Why is there a saucer of sugar under John's bed?" Jemima called to her daughter.

"There's a trail of ants all through his sleep-out."

'Dear me, what a mess!' She fussed, gingerly picking up the saucer and brushing the milling ants from her wrist as she did so.

"Margie, did you hear? There're ants all through this sleep-out"

"Marge is over at the kitchen Mum" Vera called back to her mother.

"She's getting lunch ready for the men." Vera was resting on a couch in the breeze-way, her legs elevated on cushions and a damp towel laid over her. She had been feeling the heat of late and frequently chose this spot to rest, where she benefited from any cooling draught there might be.

Jemima, stamped her feet on the floorboards as tiny ants began to swarm over her ankles. She carried the offending saucer of sugar outside onto the lawn. Here she found her grandson riding a longhaired black nanny goat. A young very dark native was leading him about the garden.

"My oh my John! Look at you" she said admiringly as she paused to watch.

"What a lovely goat. What's her name?"

John, who was still a little shy of the elderly lady who had recently come to stay with them, looked at his grandmother with huge dark eyes. He was wondering why she was holding the saucer he used for his pet ants. He had only just re-filled it that morning.

"What's your pet goat called?" Jemima asked him again. This time, approaching the animal and stretching out her free hand to stroke the long black hair. It had a large udder and judging by its comparatively clean teats, Jemima rightly assumed she was used, not only as a riding goat for the children, but also as a milker.

"What you 'bin call 'im?" the aboriginal boy coaxed, as John still sat speechless on the animal's back.

"That one's called Ginger" John said presently, pointing to where a large wether stood tethered beneath the tamarisk trees. He spoke quietly and slowly, Jemima wondering, not for the first time whether her grandson had inherited his father's distinctive drawl.

"Oh, I see. He's lovely too," his grandmother said admiringly. Then, seeing Roslyn seated in the shade with June and her own twelve month old daughter beside her, Jemima abandoned her quest for the nanny goat's name and walked across to the young native mother. This must be the infant Margaret had delivered last year in the room next to the kitchen, she supposed. She remembered her daughter saying how little liquor Roslyn had had and how relieved they were that the baby was so healthy. Jemima had heard a lot about Roslyn in her daughter's letters home. How she had been taken by Willie, one of the Sunday Island lads, to be his wife. Margaret spoke very highly of Willie and his brother Con. Con was also married, having taken over Maudie after she had lost her first husband in an accident. Jemima was pleased Margaret had written so regularly and kept her so well informed of the station happenings. It made it so much easier to come into this strange new world which she had found hard to imagine whilst in far off New England.

"Do you know where I might find a broom?" she now asked Roslyn.

"There're ants all through the sleep-out"

"Mum! What are you doing outside without your hat on" Margaret asked, coming through the gate with a bowl of mashed potato in her hand.

"There you are dear. I was just looking for a broom to sweep out John's room. Look what I found under his bed!" and she held out the offending saucer.

Margaret, who was being followed by Dora and Lulu bearing dishes of pumpkin and boiled meat, clicked her tongue with irritation.

"That's John for you Mum!" she sighed.

"Feeding the ants. He's always doing it. Leave it for now. I'll just take this in and set up, so we can have lunch." Then turning towards John she called

"That will do now Tony. You take John off that nanny goat and go and have lunch. John, run in and wash your hands. Hurry up now." Roslyn was getting to her feet, her baby slung deftly onto her hip, June clutching her other free hand.

"I'll take June in." Jemima told her.

"Come on poppet. Lunch-time" She led her bright, curly haired grand-daughter across the yard and into the house. She untied the ribbon that held a cotton bonnet securely on the two year old's head, before taking her out to the bathroom for a much needed sponge down.

Vera had already set the table and it wasn't long before the three women were seated, a child on either side of Margaret, eating the usual boiled beef, potato and mashed pumpkin. As always the meal was preceded by 'grace'.

"We thank you Lord, for these thy gifts, to our use and us to Thy service, Amen. Would you like a slice of bread Mum?" Margaret said with her usual economy of time.

"Yes please dear. Just a thin slice if you don't mind. You know Margie," Jemima spoke, somewhat tentatively,

"I see the native girls wiping themselves with the tea towels in the kitchen when they're drying the dishes. It's not right you know, to let them do that. I'll dry up for you while I'm here if you like."

"Oh what nonsense Mum." Margaret spoke impatiently.

"I've never noticed them do that, though I don't suppose I would. There's too much else to be done. But no, I don't want you doing the dishes. I'll only have to teach them to dry up again once you've gone back home. Just let things be Mum, please. I'll keep an eye on them though, if that makes you happier." She finished more gently.

"All right dear, if that's what you want." Jemima spoke placatingly.

"Who is the boy who was leading John about on the nanny-goat?" she asked, changing the subject adroitly.

"That's Tony. He's Maudie's brother. He must be a half brother I think. He's so much darker than Maudie or Freddie. They must have different fathers." She told her parent.

"Actually he's quite handy for doing little odd jobs about the place. He's a shingle short, poor boy, so George doesn't have him out in the camp. But he enjoys giving the kids rides on the goat, feeding chooks and things. He's not a bad lad, just a bit silly."

They continued eating in silence for a little, Margaret pausing between mouthfuls to help June spoon her lunch into her mouth.

"How are you feeling today Vee?" Margaret asked her sister.

"Are your ankles less swollen this morning?"

"I'm fine Marge. Don't fuss so." Vera responded.

"I promise to tell you if I'm not feeling quite the thing.

If you're not too busy, do you think we could go through those baby things this afternoon?" she asked, recalling Margaret's offer to sort through June's baby clothes for her.

"Certainly Vee. After siesta we'll have a look and see what we can find for you."

So the meal and the day progressed, as indeed did most of the subsequent days of Jemima's visit. She enjoyed being in the company of her two daughters, getting to know her grandchildren at last, both of whom soon lost their shyness and warmed to her gentle nature. The only disruptions to the daily routine of bread making, cooking, cleaning, washing and child minding were the rare but welcome visits of Don, from Blina, or George from the stock-camp,

Margaret continued to have endless chores to attend to. To add to them she had taken to preparing boiled water, which she set to cool in the meat safe. This she encouraged the young native women to take to feed to their babies from a teaspoon, being anxious to ensure the infants were kept well hydrated. Teats were impossible to obtain. She had found one that was not perished and had attached it to a bottle filled with prune juice, which she dispensed to a particularly seedy child. She was disgusted, later, to find the old men in the camp sucking the sweet dark liquid from the bottle, leaving none for the baby for whom it was intended.

It was a constant concern to Margaret how much difficulty the native women had in rearing their offspring. Their young, almost without exception, failed to thrive. In an effort to try to improve the mother's milk supply, Margaret took to giving nursing mothers rolled oats morning and evening, as well as continuing her practice of sending down bread and meat daily. Fresh fruit and vegetables were not easily obtained, nor looked upon with much favour by the aborigines, who preferred to eat only 'meat and spuds'. Goats milk was in abundant supply, but always needed boiling before use, as the gins never learned to wash the teats adequately prior to milking. The milk was soiled and used mainly for making cheese, or in tea and coffee, where the strong flavour was disguised sufficiently to make it palatable.

Meda natives going to the Derby races.

Over the years Margaret achieved a measure of success. The children, in the main, grew into healthy adults, despite their rather slow start in life. The mothers learnt the rudiments of hygiene, even if they found difficulty in believing in its importance. They learnt also who to turn to in times of sickness, calling on Margaret day or night.

CHAPTER EIGHTEEN

John

1950 – 1951

June aged three and John aged six. April 1949.

With shrieks of delight the children had finally mustered the goats and driven them to the very brink of the billabong. Scampering back and forth, mostly naked to the waist, and without exception bare footed, the small band of youngsters worked in practiced unison to bring the mob together. Now the best fun of all was to be had. Goats hate water. Somehow the children would contrive to force the animals forward into the dreaded billabong. It would, of course, be easier, probably quicker and definitely less stressful on the goats to herd the animals up the paddock, skirt the billabong and bring them back along the far side of the lake and so to the yards. But this would have deprived the fleet footed young musterers of so much enjoyment, it was an option not even considered.

Alice, June and Rita, aided by Snowy Jabanakka, pushed the main mob forward, while John and Tommy raced to wheel a couple of wethers that, in sheer panic, had broken out at the last minute. Swift, lean and agile, tanned almost as dark as his companion, John scampered across the scalding flat, running wide of the two beasts. When he judged himself a little ahead, he swung round to cut them off, and with Tommy, fleet footed and nimble, on the other flank, they successfully wheeled the errant pair of goats back to the mob.

Each of the musterers, astride their imaginary horses, coaxed the reluctant herd of goats down to the water's edge. Clicking their tongues, as they had heard the grown-up stockmen do, they jammed the goats relentlessly forward, until at last they had forced them to wade out of their depth and were able to make them swim to the other side. While in the water, some of the more exuberant boys leapt onto the backs of the largest wethers, but their weight was too much for the wretched creatures, much spluttering ensued and the riders invariably abandoned the attempt.

Once on the far side of the billabong it was a short distance past the native camp to the goats' yard. The animals, wet and disheveled, trotted along. Docile now with exhaustion, nannies, kids and wethers moved slowly after the exertion they had been subjected to.

Life for John was idyllic. His mother was constantly occupied cooking in the station kitchen, or chivvying the native girls about their chores. His father seemed to spend endless weeks out in the stock-camp and John was left in the care of his friends the 'blacks'. Sometimes he and the growing number of aboriginal children played at mustering, whilst bringing up the goats. At others they staged buck-jump shows at the yard, taking it in turns to jump on the backs of wethers and billy-goats, trying to ride them in great style, each endeavouring to out-do the others. Such pastimes were forbidden, but this did not deter the youngsters. Only when John's father 'the boss' was seen striding across the flat towards them, would they disperse, leaving the dust to settle behind them.

The goats' yard was also a favourite spot for a less energetic pastime. The collection of boab seeds. The small, hard, kidney shaped seeds were easily gathered from goats' droppings and the children could often be found gathering pocketfuls to take away and crack in the shade. Once a good number were crushed into a pannikin a delicious and much favoured snack was made.

Margaret had tried to teach John and his sister, June, to read and write during her already busy days, but the task proved hopeless. No matter how firmly she sat them down to practise their letters, the slightest distraction would see them scamper outside and away beyond her reach. Her own work, always pressing and seemingly impossible to catch up on, invariably caused Margaret to abandon the class until another day, when the same outcome resulted. In the meantime John became more and more familiar with the natives and their way of life. They took him along with them on their Sunday 'walkabouts', hunting, fishing down the river, seeking out sugar bag honey, or whatever else took their fancy. During these all day 'picnics', John was cared for and guided by them. He shared their food, cooked in coals, be it fish, goanna, kangaroo, snake, or simply a pannikin of coongleberries or a fistful of honey. He liked kangaroo the least of all, finding the flesh tough and gamey, usually only partially cooked and covered in flies. But mostly the tucker was good. The older gins, in whose charge he was generally left, looked after him with infinite care. They gave him the choicest morsels, guarded him from possible harm, and helped him bait his fishing line. They shielded him from all chance of injury, taught him how to avoid cat-fish spines, watch out for snakes lurking in tree-trunk hollows and recognize the crescent slides of crocodile on the muddy riverbanks.

Fishing was a favourite pastime of the natives. Even during the week, when most of the station was busy, Maudie would take John to dig for 'wollocks' in the wet parts of the garden, to use as bait. The frogs they dug were brown, with large heads and dark googly eyes. Maudie and the other native girls were adept at finding them, gathering them together in an old sugar bag, hopeful of ensnaring a large barramundi with the succulent creatures when they next cast a cotton line into the nearby May River. If 'wollocks' were in short supply, they dug for sand frogs instead, down at their fishing spot, breaking the hind legs to keep the creatures from escaping.

Barramundi, huge and heavy to carry the mile or so home, were abundant. Rarely did a day's fishing result in disappointment. Always eager to share what they had, the biggest and best fish was frequently hauled back to the homestead, where it was presented to Margaret. Ready gutted and scaled, she would cook it for the men in the station kitchen that night, taking some across to the house for the family. Other excess fish, caught during the day and not already consumed on the river-bank, would be carried home to the native camp and shared amongst their own people. Barramundi were not the only fish caught. There seemed to John always to be a constant supply of cat-fish to toss on the coals of their camp-fire. Sometimes cherrabun were plentiful, depending on the season, and if they were fishing the salt water reaches of the May, salmon were easily caught during the cooler months of the year. Occasionally large, heavily pincered mud crabs were collected, but they were not so popular as the smaller but sweeter fresh water crabs found in the billabongs.

When fishing down at the salt water, John was forever being chastised for sitting too close to the bank. The 'old girls' calling him to move ten or fifteen feet back from the edge.

"Lingwadda get ya" they told him, always fearful of the large saltwater crocodiles that were known to live there. He listened to their stories of how crocodiles knocked down their prey with their strong tails, before grabbing it and rolling with it under the murky water. They showed him large crescent slides, where the huge reptiles had lain, sunning themselves on the muddy bank, indentations of their jowls showing the horrific width of massive heads.

But it was not always to instill fear into his young mind that they told him of the creatures they came across during their wanderings. He was to learn where the bee-eaters nested in the sandy creek banks, in which tree hollows the cockies laid their eggs, how the bower bird constructed his playground and where to find bush plums up in the pindan. The 'station blacks' were his teachers, his guides, companions and friends. Several of the older women claimed to be John's grannies, a relationship clung to by them even into his adult years. They bestowed on him the name of 'Bunda' after Willie, who often took him hunting with spears and woomeras, made for the 'little gudia boy' by old Jimmy Brown. With Willie, John ran down wounded kangaroos and if a joey was found in the pouch it was invariably given to him. Rarely was there a time when John didn't have at least one joey hanging in an improvised sugar bag pouch at the end of his bed in the sleep-out.

Margaret did not altogether approve of the numerous pets brought home by her son. She worried constantly about fleas, ticks, and lice being brought into the house. There was little she seemed able to do about it. During John's earliest years she had found it impossible to keep a constant watch over him and took to tying him to a running chain from the washing line, to keep him from wandering out of her sight. But as he grew older she found she was grateful for the assistance of the aborigines who kept so close an eye on him. Perhaps not always occupied in pursuits she would approve of, he was nonetheless kept from harm. She found it easier to turn a blind eye to his many exploits.

It was almost the end of the season on Meda. It had been a bad year. Very little rain had fallen since the previous 'wet' and the station was suffering drought conditions. Waterholes were drying up earlier than usual. The cattle, in depressingly poor condition, became bogged as they came in to drink, often too weak to struggle from the mud surrounding the shrunken pools . George was in a sour frame of mind. He hated destroying stock, but this was now a daily task. Even the station billabong, never before known to go dry, looked certain to do so. Rain was desperately needed.

In the unusual conditions that prevailed that year numerous pied geese flocked to the tiny stretch of water below the Meda homestead. It was normal for many bird species to be drawn to the billabong at the tail end of the season when the more outlying waterholes dried up, but pied geese were not usually amongst them. Rarely seen at Meda, they were driven by the drought that gripped the whole of Northern Australia.

Each day Margaret watched small flocks of the large black and white birds fly, in formation, over the trees to settle on the ever diminishing billabong. There was not enough room on the narrow strip of water to sustain life for so many. The pied geese died there in large numbers.

John, also observing the unusual migration of the geese, was drawn to the strange new creatures appearing in such vast numbers. He could not bear to see the scores of water birds starving to death. He found the geese easy to catch and hold, weak as they were from hunger and their long flight. He decided to gather as many as he could to try and save them from starvation.

In horror Margaret watched as John made endless visits down to the water's edge. Catching two or three of the helpless creatures at a time, he carried them back to the station and shut them in the cook's old room alongside the station kitchen. He scavenged scraps of bread with which to feed them, continuing to bring up sick and dying geese until he could fit no more in the tiny room.

Each morning, when he went out to check on the poor suffering birds he had collected, he found many dead and stiff. These he threw out, counting the corpses carefully before going down to the billabong to replace them with live ones. So the pattern continued, day after day. As the geese died, so John would bring up more, trying to feed them, hoping to save lives already beyond possible recovery.

Margaret finding him covered in lice, mud caked up to his ankles and smelling appalling hustled him off each day to the ablution block for a good scrub down and de-lousing. She lived in dread of his contracting some obscure disease from so much physical contact with the birds, but try as she would, she could not impress on him the hopelessness of his task. She endeavoured to enlist the help of her husband, but George was too pre-occupied with troubles of his own, with drought stricken stock, to care much what his young son was doing.

"Mum, Mum! Look what I've got" John called to her one afternoon, startling her from her brief siesta.

"Come and see my brolgas." Still slightly drowsy from her catnap, Margaret emerged into the glare of scorching sunlight, to find John standing proudly at the foot of the steps between two fully-grown stately brolgas.

"However did you bring those in?" she asked in surprise. Despite being obviously undernourished the grey crane like birds, with impressive scarlet markings about their heads, were clearly too large for a boy his size to carry.

"Easy Mum! I led them up by their beaks," John told her with satisfaction.

"What do you think of them? Just wait till I show old Eilie and Dora"

"I think they will peck your eyes out John. Now keep away from them" his mother implored. But John was not to be parted from his new pets. They were a prize indeed and he longed to tell his friends in the camp.

He let go of the two sturdy beaks and ran to close all the gates from the house yard. He placed a container of water close by the birds and then set about begging for scraps from his mother. When none were forthcoming he snatched a handful of lush grass from beneath a leaking tap and tried to entice the birds to peck at it. The two brolgas, much to everyone's surprise, remained in the garden for quite some time. Too weak to fly, or venture far, they strutted and pecked about the lawn, becoming quite a part of the homestead scene.

John was in disgrace. He had been upsetting his sister. She had asked for it really, he reasoned. June, the beautiful, blond haired, blue eyed girl who rarely gave cause for recrimination. The only time he could recall her doing anything wrong was when she had given all her nickers, in a fit of charity, to the native children, who always went about in a state of partial or total undress. Even this had not been looked upon with too much disfavour by his parents, for although Margaret was decidedly vexed, George had swiftly pointed out the kind-hearted nature that provoked such an action. It was the same on that other occasion when she was found collecting used cigarette butts on the Indian Pacific train, when they last visited their grandmother in New South Wales. June had then persuaded her mother that she was saving them for the natives who were always short of tobacco.

John, who never found anyone willing to defend him when things went wrong, dwelt long and hard on the problem of June. Eventually he cornered his sister with a promise to tell her a terrific secret.

"So you see? You must be adopted." He told her.

"You're not really one of us at all. Not a real Wells." Gratified to see a look of doubt creep into June's expression, he tried to press his point home, saying convincingly,

"See, you've got blonde hair, pale skin and blue eyes. Mum and Dad have both got dark hair. I take after them, but you don't. It's pretty obvious really. You're adopted all right." John watched with delight the effect his words had on his sister. Her face crumpled as, red with fury, she rushed away sobbing in search of her mother, demanding to be told the truth.

John

The episode had earned John a sound chastisement. He was a child of strange and complex motivation. Whereas he enjoyed occasioning June's tearful outbursts, he could not bear to see distressed animals. He had learned to cope with the necessary slaughter that was part of the natives' way of life, but his passion for accumulating pets was always uppermost in his mind when on hunting expeditions with them. If a kangaroo was speared, there might well be a joey for him to carry home. Likewise the skinny goanna they had dug out, that was now leading a high life tethered to the stumps of the homestead verandah where John fed it copious amounts of finely chopped raw meat. What he really wanted now was a dog, all of his own.

The longed for rains had finally come. His father was confined to the homestead and was spending his days in the blacksmith's shop and garage, where engines were being overhauled and saddles repaired.

John had been eavesdropping and had overheard that his father would be going to town the next day. It sounded as though they were to be given a dog, puppy no doubt, by Ned Delower, who thought the animal would be better suited to station life than confined to town. John's active young mind had been feverishly at work. How could he persuade his stern parent to let him go into Derby with him to collect the puppy? More ambitious still, how might he convince the old man to let him keep it for his own pet? The latter seemed a very thin hope and he cursed the fact that he had so recently blotted his copybook by upsetting his sister.

Always direct and straight to the point, John decided his best approach was to ask his father outright, hoping that he might have forgotten his earlier misdemeanour.

"Can I come into town with you to collect the puppy?" John asked his father over breakfast the next morning.

"I'm not going in to collect a puppy. I'm picking up stores and I may collect the animal at the same time." George spoke sharply. He was vexed at the implication that Emanuel's precious fuel was to be used for anything other than essential journeys. Then relenting slightly he continued.

"Yes I s'pose so. But make sure you're tidied up and ready. We'll go in after smoko. I won't be waiting so don't be late."

"Righto Dad. Thanks" said John, a look of delight on his fresh young face.

Later that day father and son drove into town, a distance of thirty miles. Since the onset of the 'wet' the lower road, a sand track that ran past the Claypan, Forrest Camp, Native Well and on to Deep Well the usual route taken to Derby, was impassable. Although this road had been built up from Native Well on to Goodie Goodie, from there it ran straight across the marsh to town. If there were adverse tidal conditions, it was possible to skirt the marsh by taking a track around Devil's Point keeping to the high ground. But with the recent rains, not only was the marsh section of the road now impassable, but much of the Meda country was boggy, if not under water.

John and his father, followed the telegraph line that day. It ran through the pindan ridge, keeping to the high ground for much of the way. It was a slow laborious drive. The track wound, in zigzag fashion, between each telegraph pole and the journey took a good two hours to complete. The two occupants hardly spoke as the cumbersome vehicle lurched its way, in slalom like fashion, toward Derby. George, who was never given to idle chatter, had nothing to say to his son on the way in. John, who was bursting to ask his father if the puppy could be his, spent most of the drive trying to pluck up the courage to do so. His father, looking so stern and straight as he concentrated on the job of driving seemed as unapproachable as always. It wasn't until they were dropping off the pindan ridge, parallel to the Leprosarium, that he spoke up.

"Can the puppy be mine, Dad?" he blurted out before his courage failed.

"I'll look after it, feed it and everything." His words, almost lost in the roar of a gear change, went unheeded for several long minutes.

"We'll see." George answered. His clipped tone and terse manner discouraged John from pressing his plea further.

John

Once in the small township, they collected an assortment of provisions from MacGovern and Thompson. They called at Rowell's, the station agent, and picked up parts and the mail. With the Buick well laden they drove down the wide street to Ned Delower's house.

"Ah, good to see you," they were greeted, as they climbed from the vehicle.

"So you've come to get it then. I'm glad you're taking him. He's not a bad dog really, but not very well suited to town it seems." Mr. Delower chatted amiably as they walked across to the gate.

"Look, we haven't got the time to stop Ned" George told him.

"I'll see how he goes out there. He might turn out to be a good dog with some work. That's about all I can do I'm afraid. Now we really must not stop," and turning to John he said

"John, go and get it will you. It's time we were heading back out."

"He's chained up under the mango tree son," Ned told him, smiling broadly.

Delighted, John ran across the yard to the side of the building where a large tree shaded the fence, the branches almost touching the roof of the ramshackle dwelling. He paused mid stride to look, with considerable misgiving, at the animal chained up in front of him. He saw a large, fully grown, black and tan dog. It had a stumpy tail and was growling with hackles up, it's lip curling ferociously.

"There's only a big dog here Dad," he called back to the two men waiting by the gate.

"I can't see a puppy."

"Oh, he's no pup!" Mr Delower laughed out loud.

"I've been told to get him out of town 'cos he's been frightening folks in here."

"Just get it John!" his father said crossly.

"You wanted it, remember? Now hurry up, we haven't got all day"

John turned back to the snarling beast. He approached it cautiously and very gingerly undid the chain. The dog continued to growl viciously. John had severe doubts about it's nature. He wasn't at all sure he still wanted a dog after all.

Having successfully got the animal into the back of the Buick without being savaged, they said farewell to it's relieved owner and headed for home. During the long hot drive back to Meda John's mind was fully occupied with thoughts of his new acquisition. He pondered on the savage nature of the beast and wondered how he was going to handle it. Presently his father pulled up. It was a hot, humid day. Storm clouds were building up in the distance and rain seemed assured again that night.

In the back of the utility, the dog lay panting. There was little shade in which it could shelter from the scorching sun. John climbed down from his passenger's seat. Going to the back of the vehicle he found a tin lid and poured water into it. He offered the liquid to the dog. To his surprise all the aggression seemed to have vanished. The dog lapped the water thirstily. John put out a hand and touched it tentatively. From that moment a bond was established. Oglebash, as the creature was later named, became his inseparable companion.

From that sultry afternoon onwards, Oglebash followed John everywhere. They set off together for daylong excursions on the run. John rode a bicycle and carried a small knapsack containing billy-can, pannikin, tea and sugar. Oglebash padded along tirelessly behind. Together they hunted kangaroos, tracked snakes, found bird nests and caught butterflies. They often strayed far from the homestead and became so absorbed with what they were doing that it was, sometimes, well past sundown before they returned home.

Margaret became increasingly anxious over her son's roaming. But George would reassure her when John was particularly late, saying,

"Don't worry. He'll be back when he gets hungry," and he invariably was.

Whenever John found himself in trouble for some misdeed or

other, he was frequently able to evade the customary belting with a leather strap. Being accompanied by Oglebash almost every moment of the day no-one was able to lift a finger against him. The dog was as savage, to anyone threatening his master, as he had been when first acquired, and only John was spared it's ill nature. On the rare occasions when John was ill his faithful friend still protected him. John did not have to swallow the medicine proffered by his mother. Oglebash defended him from under the bed, forcing Margaret to retreat with the foul tasting remedy.

The breakdown in discipline caused by John's canine friend was not to be tolerated indefinitely. A despairing Margaret tackled George on the subject.

"We must do something about John," she said one evening, in the privacy of their sleep-out.

"He's eight years old. It's time he had some proper schooling."

"I thought you were teaching him Margaret" her husband replied, surprised.

"I never went to school until I was nine."

Margaret felt irritated. She paused a moment to quell the impulsive retort that sprang to her lips. Presently she said with the utmost tact,

"Yes I know George. And you left when you were twelve. But things are different now. John must have a proper education. I can't teach him here. Every time someone passes by the gate, or I get called away, John and June shoot through." She sighed. The frustration of so much wasted effort wore her down. She knew she had to pass the job over to professional educators. She was exhausted, the task seemed hopeless and there was very little to show for all her efforts.

"Well, that damn'd dog can be got rid of for starters" George stated matter of factly.

"I'll have it shot tomorrow," and with that he rolled over, turned out the lamp and settled on his pillow to sleep.

Within seconds Margaret could hear his deep rhythmic breathing. 'Out like a light and not a care on his mind' she thought resentfully. 'Tomorrow there'll be one dead dog, a furiously distraught boy to cope with and the problem of education still unresolved'.

Margaret lay awake late into the night, fretfully considering the possibilities open to her. She had already thought of moving into Derby and sending the children to school there. She had even asked Hughie Watt, a friend of theirs, whether she could use a vacant house she had heard was available. His response had both startled and surprised her.

"You certainly can't rent the house Margaret" he told her.

"It would be utterly immoral of you to leave George out on Meda to cope on his own. Even if it was vacant I would not dream of letting you use it."

Margaret, smarting at the rebuke had let the matter rest, but she was shocked by the vehemence of his refusal and the implication that she might ever consider doing anything that was wrong. The suggestion had seemed logical to her and quite proper. Now, still left with the problem of John's education, she reconsidered her options. Perhaps she should arrange for him to board in town with someone so that he could attend school there. Another possibility might be to send him down to his Aunt Nora, on the orchard, to be educated with his cousins, Wendy and Alan.

How she wished Vera was still here to talk it over with. But Don and Vera had long since left the Kimberley. Their son, Rodney, had failed to flourish and within a year of his birth, Vera, blaming the extreme heat, persuaded her husband to seek employment further south. The Bowdens had left Blina in August 1949, moving first to a station near Kalgoorlie, a year later over to Victoria. Margaret wrote frequently to her sister. She was mildly envious of Vera, now mother of two, and her amenable husband. Margaret had long since realized just how steadfast George was in his determination never to be removed from the Kimberley. Her wistful remarks to her mother, hinting at a move away from the region in three years, had long been shown to be nothing more than hopeless dreams. There would be no parting George from his beloved station. Arguments concerning June's delicate health, John's need for schooling, her need for relief from the heat, all counted for nothing with George. When Margaret felt a need to discuss a touchy subject she was met with stony silence. George would then depart, at the first opportunity, either to the stockcamp for a protracted stay, or on a bore run that would see him absent for countless hours.

It was this line of thought that eventually caused Margaret to strike on the solution to her quandary. The very fact that her husband refused to embark on any kind of heated discussion enabled her to make many decisions unhindered. If he was so reluctant to consider how John could be taught, then she felt free to decide the matter entirely herself.

With this thought uppermost in her mind, drowsiness overcame her at last. Tomorrow when she was refreshed and brighter a solution would surely present itself.

CHAPTER NINETEEN

An Education

1952 - 1956

George and Margaret had been married ten years. John, having spent a year in Derby at the primary school, had eventually been accepted into Scotch College, Perth, where he was currently boarding as one of the school's youngest and possibly most illiterate, primary students. He was nine years old and terrified. Never in his life had he seen so many boys, nor been so cold. In all his wanderings about the bush, he had never felt so lost or lonely. What could his parents have been thinking of to send him to such a place? He was teased mercilessly about his drawl. "Naap naap' was the nickname given to him and he was taunted about his tanned skin and shy nature.

Meanwhile, on Meda, Margaret was relieved beyond measure. At last she had got her son settled into a good school, where he would receive the best education available to them. It was true that the fees were exorbitant, taking half George's annual salary, but they would be able to manage somehow she felt sure. Most of their daily requirements were being provided by the station.

She had taken John down to the city herself after Christmas, staying with her mother-in-law, who lived conveniently equidistant from the city and college. Here she had set him up with the required uniform, arranged a standing order of food items at Boans Store and left an allowance of thruppence a week pocket money with his house-master. This was considered sufficient to last him until the August holidays, when he was next allowed home.

John's grandmother had baked him a large fruitcake and, together with a quantity of apples from his uncle's orchard, Margaret had deposited her son at his new school well satisfied.

She had looked with disdain at the handful of sniveling mothers leaving their offspring in the large dormitory where she had also left John. 'Whatever was wrong with them to make such a to do' she thought. 'The boys would be fine just as soon as their parents departed'. No-one would find her indulging in such an unnecessary display of emotion. With a brisk step and firm expression she left the school grounds, without a backward glance.

Margaret would not have felt so satisfied with her efforts had she been fully aware of the true situation in which she had landed her son. Those first few days had found him sick with fear. He had never seen so many other boys, most of them a good deal bigger and stronger than himself. All about him was noisy and intimidating. Traffic roared incessantly. Boys voices could be heard in every building and across the playing fields. Teachers bombarded him with instructions. John hated it. He cried himself to sleep every night, smothering his head with his pillow so that no-one would hear him. His misery a private trial to be endured alone.

During his second term at boarding school John was accommodated in the sick bay. He found the southern winters bitterly cold and he succumbed to numerous minor ailments throughout the term. He attended classes when well enough, hiding in a sunny sheltered corner of the grounds during leisure times, returning to the sanatorium at night. He longed for the warmth of the North and lived each day of his new found hell, counting them off in his diary. The two week August break, when he was to be allowed home to Meda, seemed like an impossible dream.

By the end of his first year at boarding school John was beginning to grow wise to the ways of his new world. He had learnt the expected code of behaviour necessary to be accepted by the other boys. If an older boy asked for an item from his tucker box, John gave it to him unhesitatingly. If he did not he knew he would get a flogging, after which the bigger lad would take what he wanted anyway. By the same token, John had no qualms about dealing the same treatment out to a boy smaller than he was. He felt no guilt about such bullying. Even at Meda in the fowl yard he knew there was an 'order of peck'. The strongest had first go, the weakest waited their turn for the last picking. This was the rule and he accepted it unquestioningly.

Ironically, whilst John was banished to Perth for his education, Margaret had found a new pupil to teach on Meda. Since she and George had first arrived on the station the population of the native camp had increased substantially. This was due in some measure to the birth of several children to the couples already living in the camp. A number of other individuals had moved to Meda over the years. Whether news of conditions there had encouraged this trend Margaret could only guess, but she was known to be caring and diligent in her dealings with people. At the same time both she and George were recognized as capable but hard task masters. George Wells was fair but tough. He was hardworking and expected others to be the same. But still the natives came. They came from Kimberley Downs, from Oobagooma and from Cherrabun.

Amongst the newcomers were some individuals who would more than prove their worth in the years to follow. Although there was no-one held in higher regard by the Wells' family than the unassuming Willie Lennard, the likes of Billy Munroe, July Rowley and Tommy May were all valued additions to the camp and station community. Tommy May, with his brothers, Victor and Walter, arrived on Meda to join the workforce there when Tommy was sixteen years old. Margaret and George knew them to be competent and hardworking stockmen as they had come from Cherrabun Station. Anxious to learn how to read and write, Tommy was envious of the other children who were then boarding at the Aboriginal School Hostel in Derby. Being too old to go to school with them, yet showing signs of being a willing student, Margaret decided to teach him herself. He came to the homestead in the evenings where together they sat in the lamplight poring over early readers. During these lessons numerous insects would land on the pages, swarming about the light as they worked. Literacy did not come easily to Tommy but he was a dogged pupil. He was the antithesis of Margaret's own offspring and she found it rewarding, if slow work, teaching him. For Margaret the time she spent helping Tommy proved more than worthwhile. In later years he became a community leader amongst his own people, a devout Christian and an accomplished artist, even travelling overseas, with fellow indigenous painters, to exhibit his work.

As with many of the natives on Meda, Tommy had been given his surname by Margaret and George Wells, who were directed by the authorities to allocate names to those who did not already have them. Neither Margaret nor her husband approved of this directive, but Aborigines on other properties were in a similar position and many were being given hopelessly inappropriate or undignified names. Preferring to name the Meda natives themselves, rather than leave it to others, George and Margaret set about the task as best they could.

Jimmy Bird proved the easiest to name, electing to adopt the surname of a former employer, but choosing for others was not so simple. It was presently decided that they should be named after rivers in the area. Hence Roslyn, Willie, Con, Maudie and their many children all adopted the surname Lennard, this being the largest river in the immediate vicinity of the station. Peculiarly, the lower reaches of this same watercourse, where it ran through Meda and out to sea at Point Torment, was known as the May River, after which they named Tommy. By naming the natives in this way they hoped to give them not only identity, but some added dignity, for there was a certain pride amongst them of their association with the stations on which they lived. At the annual race rounds, Aborigines from all the surrounding properties would congregate for the festivities, sporting new shirts, strides and broad brimmed hats, symbols of their station's patronage.

An Education

With the growing population on Meda, Margaret's responsibilities increased, being unofficial nurse to many of them. With the arrival of Sambo, from Oobagooma in 1953, came the responsibility of nursing his diabetic wife, Lizzie. She required daily injections of insulin. July Rowley came from Kimberley Downs in 1955, with a terminally ill husband, Bullocky Mick. Billy Munroe and his wife, Weeda, also came from Kimberley Downs, Billy proving to be a valuable stockman in the camp for many years. July was of particular interest to Margaret, for word had it that she had suffered from a broken back as a girl. Her people had buried her, up to her neck, in sand. They had fed and watered her, but left her effectively immobilized until her spine had mended. Later as a young woman she was unable to give birth in the natural way, her baby being delivered by caesarian section. Her daughter, Patsy, was a difficult child who took up all of her mother's time, rendering July unavailable for the numerous chores generally shared by the younger women in the camp. However she more than made amends in later years, coming to Margaret's aid during an influenza crisis that swept through the station community. Margaret had also been laid up in bed. Too ill to attend to even the most essential duties, she was forever grateful to July for taking on the role of cook at that time. With almost every person sick and too weak to work, July alone seemed able to rise to the occasion. She ensured that not only those in the native camp, but the 'Missus' in the homestead as well, were fed. She made a nourishing stew, served with rice or potatoes, each day until the epidemic passed and life returned to normal.

Some forty years later, as Margaret sat beside a hospital bed in the General Ward at Derby, where July Rowley lay dying, Margaret recalled those days at Meda. To the brisk young nursing staff who attended her, July was just another elderly Aboriginal patient whose time had come to leave this world. To Margaret she was a remarkable woman who had endured much suffering in her time, but with a strength and fortitude matched by few. She remembered with a secret smile the humour of July's retort one long ago morning when Margaret had chastised the native girls for keeping her sleepless till the early hours. The rains had come and, down in the camp, there was great celebration. Singing and dancing, the corroboree-ing had gone on for hours, but when Margaret had tried to tick them off for their thoughtlessness next morning, July had laughed.

"What Missus? You 'bin want us like 'dem chooky-chook? Go to bed longa' sundown, an' get up 'longa chooky- chook daylight."

Margaret sat for sometime, quietly holding the thin black hand while her mind drifted back over the years. How times had changed. How these people had altered. How fortunate she had been to know the likes of this wonderful old woman. Margaret prayed for the soul of her former friend, before quietly leaving the room. Two days later July Rowley was dead.

After the initial years on Meda, when Margaret had found it difficult to adjust to her role of wife and mother, cook and caregiver, the subsequent decade and a half seemed less obviously punctuated with highs and lows. With John approaching adolescence within the safe confines of his Perth school and June likewise bound for a southern education, Margaret devoted herself to an existence of hard work without the pressing worry of 'outback teacher' embarked upon by many other station wives.

Although conditions had slowly improved over the years, with the installation of a small generator, a decent sanitary system and improved cooking arrangements in the station kitchen, Margaret still found her life fraught with unexpected difficulties. Of these the delivery of yet another baby was one of the most memorable.

Lucy, a highly intelligent native girl, had not long been living on Meda. She was already the mother of several children and was well established in labour when she presented to Margaret. The delivery was uneventful, but Margaret was aghast when Lucy suffered a massive post-partum haemorrhage. Frantic with worry over her patient's considerable blood loss, Margaret telephoned the doctor in Derby. She followed his advice to 'ballot' the uterus, waiting with some anxiety for the arrival of a taxi to convey Lucy and her newborn infant to the native hospital thirty miles away. Some days later Margaret telephoned to enquire after her patient's condition and was surprised to learn Lucy's previous medical history. It was revealed that Lucy had suffered significant bleeds in the past, after giving birth to her previous children. As a result of this Lucy had been able to provide the hospital staff with a card giving details of her blood group which she had apparently packed in her small carrybag. This had enabled hospital staff to proceed without delay to transfuse her, whereupon she had made a good recovery.

The dramatic events of Margaret's life were not all related to nursing. Surprises of a very different nature were frequently in store for her. One evening, while she was fast asleep, the unexpected swaying of the iron-framed bed suddenly woke her.

"Have you let the dog in the house George?" she asked with some indignation.

"I can feel it rubbing its back up and down under the bed." She propped herself up on her elbow.

"That's not the dog, Margaret" George told her calmly

"It's an earthquake."

The bed was still swaying slightly as Margaret leapt up. The cups were rattling on their hooks on the dining room dresser. She heard a strange clicking noise that, she later realized, was the brush for the fridge flue swinging back and forth on it's nail. Strangest of all was the sound of water sloshing from side to side against the walls of the cement tank. It was an odd sensation to feel the uneasy shuddering of the homestead. She turned to her husband and placed a gentle hand on his arm. The rhythmic sound of his breathing told her he was already sound asleep, apparently unperturbed by the phenomenon she found so fascinating.

A more frightening experience, it not being a freak of nature, but something much more sinister, was the unexpected blast from the Montebello bomb. Margaret was puzzled to hear what sounded like thunder, when there was no evidence of a storm looming. Two of the station inhabitants, Hellfire Jack and Lucy, were camping out bush at the time and felt the effects of the blast far more strongly than those in at the homestead. Margaret listened, with keen interest, to the couple's account of the experience when they returned somewhat shocked, to the station after the event.

"I was having a bogey at the time, Missus" Lucy told her

"And the water in the billabong went from side to side in a great wave." The eyes in her dark face were wide with wonder.

"The chains on the tractor were rattling and the dogs went proper silly. Runnin' about an' barking. We heard the blast Missus' but thought it was an earthquake at first. Then we didn't know what to think."

"I'm sure you didn't Lucy" Margaret told her.

"I thought it was thunder, but there were no clouds about. It seemed very odd. Anyway, we know now. Quite a stir it's caused. All in the news and that. Now Lucy, here are some stores for you to take when you go back out. Don't forget the spuds and onions I put ready, will you?" Margaret told her, settling back into the routine of normal daily life once more.

In 1955 Margaret became gravely concerned about her husband's health. He had not taken a holiday of any sort for five years. His spare frame was leaner than ever, his skin taut across his cheekbones. He was tetchy and awkward, the strain of too many long and difficult seasons telling in his every action.

"You simply must take a holiday George" Margaret told him firmly,

"You look like death. I know how much the station means to you, but it's not worth killing yourself for." She added bluntly.

" I am booked to go over East to see Mum next month. I realize you can't accompany me then, but I think you should fly over once the rains have come. You've never been and the change will do you good."

Throughout their marriage Margaret had assumed the upper hand in matters concerning the health of her family. Although it might have seemed to others that she was the stronger partner of the two, this was not the case. George was decidedly determined and in control, when he wanted to be, and only allowed Margaret to have her way when he chose to do so. If what Margaret said clearly held merit George was not averse to listening. He might not respond immediately, but after due consideration frequently complied with her wishes. Such was the case on this occasion. George knew himself to be weary and rundown and he agreed to the plan outlined by his astute wife.

Margaret travelled to Guyra as arranged, just prior to the 'wet' of 1955. George flew across some weeks later, after the onset of the rains, having satisfied himself that Meda had received sufficient falls to ensure the wellbeing of the stock during his absence.

It proved a successful holiday. He enjoyed meeting his brother-in-law, Don Bowden, again, who had by then brought Vera to her home town. They lived next door to 'Roslyn' with their two sons, enabling Vera to look after her elderly mother, Jemima, who was then eighty-two years old. Don had left his life on the land and found work in Guyra. He and George had a lot to catch up on. They spent countless hours talking about the Kimberley and their mutual acquaintances there. Together they travelled about the district of New England, attending sheep dog trials and visiting local agricultural shows. Don showed George the undulating farming region around Armidale. There was much for the Kimberley cattleman to see. He surprised Margaret with his eagerness and interest. She liked nothing more than sitting talking to her mother and sister, enjoying the cooler climate and walking down town on the odd errand. Meanwhile George caught buses and trains to the neighbouring towns of Glen Innes, Inverell, Uralla or Warialda, seeing as much as he could and making the very most of the weeks he had to spend in the region.

After twelve years of marriage he met, for the first time, Margaret's brother Bill Coakes and found him likeable and less pious than his sisters. Bill worked for the local Shire and had little in common with George, but they enjoyed the occasional visit to the hotel together and a mutual respect was established between them. George was amused to find this only son of Jemima's to have ginger hair and a fair complexion. He had not forgotten Margaret making such a fuss of the fact that his own father had similar colouring and how little she thought of it. Bill was a quick tempered young man, clearly the victim of two bossy sisters, but obviously held in high regard by the townsfolk amongst whom he seemed to have limitless friends.

All in all it was an eye opening experience for George. He had never ventured out of Western Australia since his arrival there as a very young child in 1904. The visit to New South Wales gave him much to think about over the coming years and he returned there several times during the remaining years of his life.

Revitalised and refreshed, he and Margaret journeyed home together to take up the reins of management once more on Meda, where they remained for another decade.

CHAPTER TWENTY

Stumpy Fraser

1960 - 1964

George Wells, who was now in his early sixties, was looking forward to a good season. Over the years he had built up a staff of fine, dependable men. Some had been reared on the station, while others had joined him later from other properties. Amongst these was his current headstockman, Fred 'Stumpy' Fraser, who had joined the Meda staff the previous season.

Although stockwork was of the first importance to George and undoubtedly his greatest interest, he was also an excellent bush mechanic. Now, in the latter years of his working life, he frequently found that his contribution in the workshop fixing engines, or out on the run attending to the bores, was of more value to the smooth running of Meda than drafting cattle in the choking dust of the stockyards.

George had full confidence in the ability of his present head stockman, who had run an efficient and effective camp for him during the previous season. Stumpy Fraser had come to Meda from nearby Yeeda station, bringing his family with him. Already acquainted with the Wells' they had once lived on a rugged and isolated station in the King Leopold Ranges, known as Mount Hart. Stumpy's three children Kevin, Gail and Ross, although a few years younger than John and June, were already accomplished horsemen, having assisted their father from a young age. In earlier years, when passing through Meda droving cattle from Mount Hart to Broome,

Margaret would ply the young Frasers with lemon squash and cake, a treat they enjoyed. The family had made an interesting spectacle droving their stock through the station, using a camel team to carry their supplies, instead of the usual pack horses or mules.

***Yoking the mules at Meda. 'Stumpy' Fred Fraser
and Aboriginal helper 'Spider' (standing)***

The Frasers' arrival at Meda in 1960 had been welcomed, not only by George, but also by his daughter June, who found the three children wonderful companions. They were all amiable and caring and seemed to June to be mature beyond their years. Together, the foursome devised games, competitions and a variety of often exhilarating, though perhaps not always approved of, amusements. They became June's good friends when she came home from Perth for school holidays.

It was late May 1961. The season was off to a good start. The horses had been mustered early, drafted, gelded and the youngsters broken in. Mustering had commenced on schedule and the stockcamp, under Stumpy's supervison, was currently out at Yuringa putting sale cattle together for a forthcoming shipment. Things were going well. Stumpy could not foresee any undue difficulty in meeting the required numbers by the specified date.

The head stockman, today accompanied by his eldest son Kevin, a youth under his care named Albert and a number of experienced ringers, including Billy Munroe, was cutting out sale cattle on the Yuringa flat close to the Meda River. They had about five beasts left to cut out for the sale mob. One of these, a young nobby bull, had no sooner been cut out by the stockmen than it doubled back and headed into the main mob again. Stumpy, annoyed, rode in immediately and proceeded to cut it out a second time. He was riding a smart young camp mare named Vanity. Especially trained for this specific job, she was an intelligent, good looking bay. As with the other camp horses, she was only ever used for the purpose of camp drafting and was never ridden during the long arduous days of mustering, for which most working horses are kept.

Stumpy was an accomplished horseman and, together with Vanity, soon had the young bull separated once more from the main group of cattle. However, it did not run into the waiting group of sale cattle as intended, but instead headed for the bush and freedom. Stumpy Fraser, unwilling to lose the animal, rode off in pursuit. Chasing it across the flat he raced alongside and started to shoulder it. The bull propped, putting his head down under Vanity's girth. He lifted the mare, causing horse and rider to fall. Vanity landed on top of her rider crushing him to the ground.

Witnessing the fall from a short distance away, members of the stockcamp rode quickly over to assist. The bull had gone, Vanity got to her feet, shook herself and stood trembling nearby. Stumpy continued to lie motionless where he had fallen. The men lifted him gently and carried him over to the camp. Placing Stumpy carefully on his swag Kevin and young Albert were instructed to ride with all haste back to the homestead for help. The more experienced members of the camp, sensing the seriousness of the man's injuries were anxious for the boys to be removed from the scene. The two young men set off on horseback in the direction of Meda with little loss of time.

Janet Wells

Several hours later, back at the homestead, George was surprised to see two stockmen riding towards him. Their horses had clearly been ridden hard. He waited with a vague sense of unease as the young men approached. Kevin Fraser quickly told his boss of the accident that had befallen his father, stating that he did not look too good and would they please take a run out and pick him up. Albert, who had accompanied Kevin, sat in silence during this exchange looking weary.

George hastened across to the station kitchen where Margaret was preparing the next meal.

"Stumpy's taken a fall Margaret. Can you put some things together and we'll drive out and fetch him" he told her briefly.

"Where is he?" she asked, memories of George's fall at Rarriwell flashing through her mind.

"The camp's still at Yuringa . The boys rode across country, but we'll have to go the longer way round. Now, I'll get the vehicle ready while you fetch what we need."

A short time later they were on their way. A mattress, pillows, blankets and bandages, hastily gathered were in the back. Margaret tried to relax in the passenger seat. With George beside her, adept at driving and with a perfect knowledge of the run, she felt less apprehensive than on that previous mercy mission she had embarked on so many years before. George sat stern and silent beside her as they proceeded along the route.

When they arrived at the stockcamp they found that the cattle had been yarded and the horses, hobbled out, were grazing nearby. Around the campfire the group of stockmen sat waiting silently. Margaret, glancing towards the still figure of their headstockman could see immediately that the case was hopeless.

The dead man was lifted onto the back of the vehicle. Margaret climbed in and settled herself beside him. As George started to drive back to the homestead she rolled a small towel and propped it under Stumpy's chin. She closed his eyes and pulled a blanket over him.

Behind them stood the remainder of the stockcamp, watching the diminishing vehicle, partially obscured by a small cloud of dust rising from the back wheels, slowly disappear.

It was a sombre drive back to the homestead, with barely a word spoken. George, never loquacious, seemed more withdrawn than ever. Apart from a few terse instructions given to Billy Munroe, whom he left in charge of the camp, he said nothing.

Once at Meda, Margaret told George to proceed on into Derby with the dead stockman. She walked indoors and headed for the nearest chair. Her legs gave way beneath her and she sat trembling with reaction. She bent her head over her knees, breathing deeply and slowly in an effort to regain some composure. Presently she felt strong enough to stand and crossed to the telephone. She made two calls, one to the hospital and one to the police station. This done she went to break the news to the Fraser family.

Over the following days it seemed to Margaret that George had taken the accident to heart. It was as if it were an affront to him personally, to his dedication, his good management, to his overriding concerns for the station and it's people. Margaret conveyed some of her anxiety to her son when she telephoned John a few weeks after the funeral. John was now a young man of eighteen, working as a brickies labourer in Perth. He had left Scotch College at sixteen and successfully completed two years at Narrogin Agricultural College. Having become disillusioned with farming, after a disastrous experience on a Pingerup property soon after leaving college, he moved to the city. He was working as labourer to five brickies at this time. It was a well paid job that satisfied his boundless energy.

The telephone conversation with his mother unsettled him. His love of the Kimberley and his life long yearning to join the cattle camps of the North proved too great a temptation. He relinquished his well paid job in the city and returned North to help his father on Meda. His wage was greatly reduced. He earned six pounds as a junior stockman, but he was marvellously happy to be home and Margaret was heartened to have her son closer at hand to help buoy up her despondent husband.

John was not yet an accomplished horseman, although he had been in the saddle on and off since childhood. He found himself being pampered and carefully guided by the native stockmen in the camp, who, with Stumpy's death still vivid in their minds, were fearful of a similar fate befalling the bosse's son. John was acutely aware of his lowly status, noting how Snowy Jabanakka, his former playmate, could ride the station 'outlaw', whilst he himself was given a string of quiet old workers, known to be the safest in the plant.

From a young lad John, while boarding in town for his early schooling, knew when the Meda cattle were at Myall's Bore ready for shipment. He would wag school for the day and ride behind the mob across the marsh to the jetty. His father would send an old pensioner, ready saddled and bridled, especially for John to ride and even then he dreamed of the days when he could become a full time stockman.

Later, during school holidays, Willie Lennard had taken to teaching John the finer points of riding for long days in the saddle. Telling him to lengthen his stirrup leathers, or loosen his horse's head, Willie had been present when John finally rode his first colt. Although Billy Munroe later taught John much about horsemanship, it was Willie who got him started and to whom John turned when he had a particular problem.

John remained in the stockcamp on Meda for the rest of that season and the following one. He began to show considerable promise and George, despite being terse and uncompromising toward his son, reluctant to show any kind of favouritism, was nonetheless pleased to have him in the camp.

Margaret was not alone in her concern for her husband. His employees, the Emanuels, also saw the change in George, which increased with each passing season. The years of hard work, long hours in the saddle and of inhaling the fine acrid dust of the stockyards, had all taken their toll on George. He no longer looked the fine strong man of his youth. With his lessening strength came a shortening of his temper. A diminishing of his humour that made life on Meda difficult for both Margaret and it's owners. It became apparent to them that something would have to be done. George was trying to work as if he was young and was still as loyal to the company as ever. The problem seemed pressing but difficult. He had worked the station as if it were his own. He had cared for the stock as though they belonged to him and repaired and salvaged equipment to spare Emanuel Brothers every expense possible. Now that the time for his retirement approached no-one could imagine how it was to be achieved without breaking his heart.

John had moved on to work as headstockman on Kimberley Downs for Messrs. Rowell and Maxted. June was doing her nursing training in Darwin. George Pollard was employed by Emanuel Brothers as assistant manager on Meda. George Wells was sixty- four years old when he was retired by the company. He was devastated, Margaret inordinately relieved. Together they had run the station for twenty years. They had built up a sound relationship of trust and respect with its' people. The native staff, who had been living there when George and Margaret first arrived from Cherrabun, had remained with them for the two decades of their management. Many others had arrived from neighbouring stations over the years. The regard in which the 'boss and his Missus' were held was high, almost to the point of awkwardness. Any proposed absences of the family from Meda had to be kept as secret as possible in an effort to avert a night of grieving by the Aborigines. If they knew that one of the family was going away there would be much wailing down in the native camp. Likewise if a Wells returned after a prolonged absence corroborees were held late into the night. George and Margaret's permanent departure from the station was a matter that all parties endeavoured to conceal for as long as possible.

The day finally came, as it inevitably had to, in 1964, when George Pollard took over the reins of management on Meda.

*Margaret Wells handing out Christmas cake to the
Aboriginal workers at Meda station. 1963.*

CHAPTER **21**

Retirement

1964 – 1962

Margaret, thinking it best to make a clean break from their previous life, took her husband on a much needed holiday to Perth. She considered he would pine less if he had the hustle and bustle of the city to distract him. George's mother Martha, was at this time, being cared for in a nursing home having suffered two fractured femurs, and, being eighty-six years old, she was unlikely to be able to return home. The house in Nedlands had been rented out, so George and Margaret went to stay with Nora and Arch. Arch Douglas had also retired and he and Nora, having left the orchard, were then living in Mount Pleasant, a riverside suburb of Perth.

Margaret took the opportunity, at this time, to do a refresher course in nursing at Osborne Park Hospital. Much had changed in the years since she had last been employed as a registered nurse and although she was a master at improvisation, showing sound common sense in her bush nursing, she knew it was not sufficient to gain her a hospital posting. She was almost fifty years old and found the modern methods of administering drugs and the extensive use of pharmaceuticals difficult to grasp. However, her knowledge and experience in midwifery stood her in good stead and she more than held her own in this area of the course. She persevered with the harder aspects of modern nursing, improving what skills she could, knowing that it was vital for her to be able to contribute to their income over the coming years.

Although the Wells' had received full board and keep along with their wage from Emanuel Brothers, they had very little money to retire on, having spent half of George's annual earnings on John's education and the remaining half on June's. The money Margaret received as station cook had been their only spending money during those years. It was now imperative that Margaret find a job.

She had first thought to seek work in Perth, where there were numerous hospitals to apply to, but George did not settle well there.

For him the wrench of leaving Meda and his beloved cattle was hard to endure. Distance did not lessen the hurt and he became morose and lethargic. Concerned for his well being, Margaret sought the advice of a doctor.

"Your husband is depressed Mrs. Wells. You should take him back North as soon as you can. I am sure he will make a full recovery there." he told her.

Margaret, alarmed at the apparent decline in her husband's health, heeded the advice she had been given. The couple set forth once more on the long journey back to the West Kimberley.

Many years earlier George and Margaret had bought a tiny corrugated iron cottage in Derby. Unlined and immensely hot, it had been occupied over the years by a retired book-keeper from GoGo Station, known affectionately as 'Old Buck"

The dwelling comprised of a minute sitting room, a shower room and a fly-screened sleep-out, which George and Margaret used as a bedroom. A narrow passage running across the back of the building acted as a kitchen and there was a small verandah at the front of the house.

By no means luxurious, George and Margaret were thankful to have the modest home in Derby in which they could retire. Being small, it required next to no furnishing, which was just as well since they owned very little. A couple of iron beds, a small table, a couch and a few footstools, made from old packing cases, seemed sufficient.

The house in Neville Street, Derby, that George and Margaret retired to after leaving Meda station.

Situated close to the Derby marsh, and having large shutters on three sides, it could be relatively cool when breezy. The property was surrounded by a vitex hedge, it's garden brightened by pink and white vinkas, frangipani trees and tachomas. It was shaded by mango and raintrees, where peaceful doves warbled and honey-eaters fed. In his latter years George took to sitting on the small verandah, enticing the birds to take titbits from his hand and feeding the shakey paw lizards tiny morsels of cooked chicken.

Not one to be inactive for long and needing something to occupy his mind, George secured a position at the local meatworks, where he worked on a seasonal basis on the cattle race. This proved fortuitous for both himself and the Derby Meat Company. It gave him some much needed contact with the stations and their stock and he was adept at deciphering the many different brands and earmarks that determined ownership of each beast killed.

Having spent a life-time working cattle, his experienced eye told him at a glance more about each beast entering the 'knocking box' than most men could glean in an hour. He was avidly interested in the condition, age, sex and nature of stock from the various stations, there being amongst them scrub bulls, shelly old cows, large sleek bullocks, old piker bullocks and poll and horned cattle of all types. They came from a vast area and George's keen eye told him much about where they had originated. Their ear-marks proved legal ownership, but he also knew if they had been mustered from the 'back country' or off the plains, from the rugged outlying stations in the ranges or the richer river country. He could pick out 'strangers' in the mob with uncanny swiftness that always ensured the rightful owner got paid.

George loved his work and it suited him well. The Demco abattoir operated from March or April until October each year, with a shut down period over the 'wet'. This enabled George to recuperate before the next season and he was able to continue working in this way until in his mid-seventies, his working life finally finishing in 1976.

Meanwhile Margaret had obtained work at Derby District Hospital, less than five minutes walk from their tiny dwelling. She was employed as Night Sister initially and was thankful, during her first few weeks back on the ward, to have the help of a kind nurse called Val Longdon while she tentatively polished up long forgotten skills.

With only two nursing staff on duty at night the women were kept busy caring for the hospital patients, one occasion seeing them tending to thirteen children in one room, all with gastro-enteritis, as well as monitoring the progress of two maternity patients.

Margaret enjoyed her return to her chosen career. She felt she was doing a worthwile job and she knew a great many of her patients. It was hard work, but never dull. She had great admiration for Dr. Lawson Holman, with whom she worked closely, although she was surprised one night when he asked her to leave the ward and attend a patient at the police station.

Retirement

"I cannot possibly do that" she told him.

"Matron has absolutely forbidden me to leave the hospital while I am on duty and I told her I wouldn't dream of doing so."

Dr. Holman told her that the police had brought in a man in a very agitated state and he wanted her to give him a needle to sedate him. He insisted she go.

"In that case Dr. you must stay here until I get back" she told him and reluctantly went to the police station to do as she was bid.

"Where is the patient?" she asked upon her arrival.

"He is in the bridal suite" they told her.

"There's no light in the room"

Margaret, always prepared, had taken a torch with her and instructing one policeman to wait outside the door, she took the second one with her into the cell. There stood a tall strong looking white man, stark naked and clearly shaking with rage.

"I have something to help you" she told him, without batting an eyelid, and proceeded to give him the injection without fuss.

"What has the man done to be in such a state?" she later asked.

"He put sugar in a prominent pastoralist's petrol tank and we were called to arrest him." She was told. Why he was stripped naked Margaret never discovered and could only assume it was all contrived to unnerve her and provide some entertainment for the men. Satisfied that she had lost none of her normal composure she hoped the prank had proved disappointing.

As well as doing night duty at the District Hospital, Margaret was also asked to work for a time at the Native Hospital down by the marsh. Being too far to walk Margaret got a taxi at ten o'clock each night to take her to work, a nun bringing her home at six in the morning. George was annoyed at the hours his wife was working and refused to co-operate with driving her. The days were very hot and, in the little iron house, Margaret found it difficult to sleep well enough to be refreshed and ready for duty the following evening.

The Native Hospital consisted of two army Nissan huts left after the war. Male patients were accommodated in one and women in the other. Children often came into the Native Hospital with their relations. Finding them difficult to control while she was busy, Margaret would pop them into bed with their uncles, grand-fathers or whoever was able to console them, leaving her free to deliver a new baby or attend to other pressing duties. By day the native patients were cared for by the nuns

Following a bad car accident in Broome in which one nursing nun was killed and another badly injured, the Medical Officer decided to close the Native Hospital due to the shortage of staff. Margaret was instructed to go and discharge as many patients as she could. Those remaining were transferred to the District Hospital where white patients were also sent home to make room for them.

"Why send me?" Margaret asked, knowing it would not be an easy task.

"Because you know most of them, you know where they live and you have a pretty good idea of their medical condition" he told her.

Margaret obeyed her instructions. The two remaining and recently bereaved nuns watched on, weeping, as Margaret sorted the patients out

In 1966 George's mother, Martha, died and to Margaret's surprise she learned that the house in Clifton Street had been left to her husband. She could foresee that this might prove fortuitous in coming years should declining health make a move south necessary.

No sooner had life settled back to normal after Martha's demise than Margaret's own mother became desperately ill. Jemima was diagnosed with ovarian cancer and Margaret hastened to New South Wales to be by her side. Jemima, naturally, was in considerable pain, on oxygen and in hospital. No sooner had her eldest daughter arrived at her bedside than Jemima demanded to be taken home.

"You promised you would nurse me at home when my time came" she reminded Margaret.

"I know I did, but you are on oxygen mother and you need to be in hospital to have that" she told her ailing parent.

"Then take me off oxygen and I will do without" Jemima responded with feeling.

Jemima was discharged into the care of her daughter who took her home to 'Roslyn' in Guyra. One week later, in August 1966, Jemima Coakes passed peacefully away, aged ninety-one. Margaret, Vera and Bill laid her to rest in the hillside cemetery overlooking the New England countryside where she had spent her entire life.

When Margaret returned to Derby she was assigned to the Outpatient's Department where she was sister in charge for the next fourteen years. During her time in this area of the rapidly expanding hospital she became extraordinarily well known, not only by the grateful townsfolk whom she tended so diligently, but also by the medical staff, who, whilst acknowledging her dedication and unquestioned ability, did not always appreciate her forthright manner.

"Would you like to see the patient in here now, or in the mortuary later?" she asked one tardy doctor.

On other occasions, if she felt a doctor had missed something during a consultation with a patient, she would discreetly knock on his door

"Excuse me doctor, but the patient you have just seen has 'such and such'. What he needs is 'such and such' I stopped him on his way out and told him you wanted to see him again tomorrow." The doctor, needless to say, found this behaviour unusual, but Sister Wells was often right and despite being annoying her conduct was helpful to them.

Margaret Wells, whilst Outpatients Sister, holding her baby grand-daughter Adele Wells, with her husband George. 1979.

Some of the more unorthodox practices of earlier years ceased as the town and hospital expanded. The occasions when Margaret was asked by Dr. Holman to step up onto the back of a utility to suture or needle someone's dog became less frequent. This pleased Margaret.

On one occasion a man was brought into outpatient's off the back of a truck, suffering from heatstroke. Unable to get a doctor to attend him for several hours Margaret plied him with wet towels from the water cooler, until he revived. When the doctor finally assessed the man he declared him fit and well enough to be sent on his way.

"You will do nothing of the sort" Margaret intervened.

"He will relapse immediately if you send him back out in this heat. He needs at least twenty-four hours on the ward"

After this incident Sister Wells, as she had become known by then, was summoned to the Matron's office.

"Would you like to retire?" the matron asked her.

"Certainly not. I am saving up to buy a new car" Margaret replied

"I won't be retiring just yet."

She continued running, as some said, 'a tight ship' in Outpatients, successfully seeing out two subsequent matrons, before finally retiring from the hospital in 1980. She was then aged sixty-five.

The same year that saw Margaret's nursing days come to an end, saw also the eightieth birthday of her husband George, and the birth of their youngest grandchild, who was named after him.

Margaret stood at the gate and watched the early model Holden Kingswood pull up in the shade of the bauhinia tree.

"Here, hand the baby to me" she said, as her daughter-in-law tried to juggle a nappy bag and infant whilst closing the car door.

"Thanks Grandma. How are you?" the young mother enquired, passing her son across.

"Well I'm busy packing up you know. I'm getting ready to die and it's nearly killing me!" her mother-in-law stated seriously. Laughing out loud, her visitor stored up this ridiculous remark for later recounting to her husband John.

"Pop is inside resting on the couch" Margaret continued

"Go on in and have a seat. Would you like a lemon squash?"

They made their way inside the small corrugated iron building.

An oscillating fan perched on a homemade stool purred rhythmically, blowing cool air toward George who now sat up on his couch.

Elderly though he was he still showed traces of his previous strength. His hands, long fingered and surprisingly large for a man of his age, showed great gentleness as he reached out to touch his new grandson. George loved these visits. Since finishing work he had little to do but reflect on the past and he was feeling contented with the way life had worked out. Now that Margaret too had retired, his days were not so lonely as they had been, and the couple were able to get about a bit more.

June, who had married in the Territory and now had three fine boys was living on a cattle station towards Mataranka. She had visited her parents recently and was lucky to be in Derby for the unexpectedly early arrival of young George, whom she had helped name. It had been an altogether happy visit.

John was now living on Meda. He had spent several years working in stockcamps before managing Napier Downs Station and later Myroodah, Kalyeeda and Lulugui. His life had had a few ups and downs but seemed to have worked out well enough in the end, George thought.

"What is John up to?" his father now asked

"Oh – he's busy as usual Pop. They're starting trapping and he's been fixing up spears and checking the waterholes. They're pretty much dry now, so he's hoping they'll do well. Tim Emanuel and Frank Mugford are coming up soon and we've got old Harry Scrivener with us fixing up saddles and making hobble straps."

George listened attentively. He liked to know of the goings on at Meda. John and his family had been there two years now. They lived in a new transportable homestead, the old house being quarters for the headstockman. Things had changed greatly since George and Margaret's time and living conditions seemed to have improved. There were ceiling fans in the main house and station kitchen and the lighting plant ran most of the time. Cooking was done on gas stoves and powdered milk was supplied instead of keeping goats.

Retirement

Although most of the people living on Meda in George and Margaret's time had now died or moved away, there were still some there that George knew. Willie Lennard and his wife Roslyn had stayed with John as he moved from station to station and were happy now to be back on Meda under his management. Jack Shaw, who had helped George and Margaret move down to Meda from Cherrabun many years earlier, was also living there and working as windmill man. He was now married and was father to a prodigious family. Freddie Marker was tending the gardens and although his sister, Maudie, now lived in Derby, as did Billy Munroe and Weeda, George and Margaret saw them often.

With their only son now managing Meda for Emanuel Brothers, bringing George news of his beloved station and it's stock on a regular basis, his declining years were brightened in the only way they could be. Margaret cared for him tenderly, nursing him through a severe case of chicken pox at the age of eighty and taking him to the comparative coolness and comfort of Clifton Street in Perth each wet season. She also took him on unexpectedly luxurious cruises to such places as Fiji, Vanuatu and once to Singapore. On alternate years they visited Vera and Don Bowden in Guyra and Alice Hall in Sydney.

George celebrated his ninetieth birthday in Derby and two years later a small group of close friends gathered on the front verandah of the Clifton Street house in Perth to celebrate George and Margaret's golden wedding anniversary.

The apple blossom hibiscus, growing at the corner of the well oiled verandah, obscured much of the party, but several passers by paused on the pavement to smile at the proceedings. Cameras clicked as the principal characters stood patiently but unnaturally behind the celebration cake. The scene was as expected and normal as any anniversary might be. Only those present appreciated the road this particular couple had travelled.

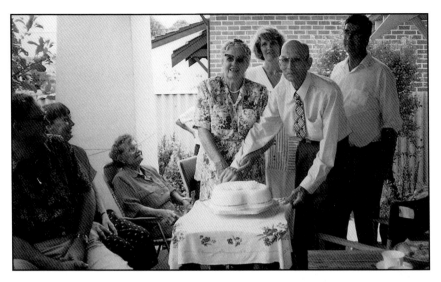

*George and Margaret's 50th Wedding Anniversary celebration,
on the front verandah at Clifton Street, Nedlands.*

*Standing L-R. Margaret Wells, June Earley,
George Wells, and John Wells. February 1992.*

Margaret Wells, aged 86, on her front verandah at Neville Street, Derby.

EPILOGUE

Margaret lost her husband, George, just before his ninety-third birthday after a short illness. Tim Emanuel gave the eulogy at his funeral service at Karrakatta Cemetery, whilst flags flew at half mast in Derby where a memorial service was held.

Margaret continued to live in the little tin house in Derby, staying at the Nedlands house for the summer months only. She took a trip to Ireland with her brother Bill in 1994 to see the country where her stalwart grandmother Margaret Jamieson originated. It seems ironic that Margaret, such a strict teetotaller, should be descended from the makers of Jamieson's Irish Whisky, which is still famous today.

Margaret's sister Vera and brother-in-law Don Bowden continued to live on Malpass Street in Guyra, next door to Jemima's old home of 'Roslyn', until 2004 when ill health forced a move to Queanbeyan in the A.C.T. to be closer to their daughter. Don Bowden is now ninety seven years old and Vera eighty seven. Margaret's brother Bill Coakes is still living on Malpass Street.

Willie and Roslyn Lennard are living in Derby and both attended the civic afternoon tea given by the Shire of West Kimberley to farewell Margaret.

Margaret Wells left Derby on October 15th 2004, exactly sixty-five years after her arrival in the West Kimberley. She will be ninety years old in February 2005 and is still in full command of 'her ship'.

ABOUT THE AUTHOR

Janet Wells

B orn in England in 1951, the author and her twin brother are the youngest children in a family of five. Her father, a biologist, and her mother, a cousin of children's author and illustrator May Gibbs, gave Janet and her siblings an idyllic rural upbringing in East Devon. Janet was educated at Sibford, a Quaker school in Oxfordshire, before attending a domestic science college and a secretarial college in Devon.

Janet travelled alone to Australia, by sea, at the age of twenty two for a two year working holiday encompassing Fiji, New Zealand and Western Australia where she met, and subsequently married, her husband John Wells, a third generation Kimberley cattleman.

She spent twenty years living in the West Kimberley, ten of them at Meda Station where her husband had grown up.

During her time in the Kimberley the author wrote two books of poetry, both published by Hesperian Press, in Perth. The first book **'Caught Off Guard and Other Poems'** was published in 1986 and reprinted in 1987. The second book, **'Waiting For Rain'** was published in 1991.

In 1994 Janet, John and their two children moved to the South West of Western Australia where they now live on a farm at Capel. Janet has busied herself with a small silk painting business 'A Touch of Silk' where she spends much of her time indulging in her love of painting flowers and birds on silk. Along the way she has found the time to write her third book **'Ready For Anything'** which is published to celebrate the nintieth year of her mother-in-law, Margaret Wells' life.

In both her writing and painting endeavours Janet has drawn heavily on her observations of the diverse environments in which she has lived. She acknowledges that she is indebted to both her parents for instilling in her a deep awareness of her rural surroundings as a child and the benefits of expressing that awareness, in one form or another, as an adult. Janet describes her poems as pictures painted with words. In this book 'Ready For Anything' she has endeavoured to paint a portrait and a landscape on the same canvas. She trusts it has worked and gives pleasure to the reader.